Child Development and Individually Guided Education

Glenn E. Tagatz

Marquette University

Addison-Wesley Publishing Company
Reading, Massachusetts • Menlo Park, California
London • Amsterdam • Don Mills, Ontario • Sydney

This book and the correlated films and filmstrips are in the
Leadership Series in Individually Guided Education,
Herbert J. Klausmeier, Editor.
Development of this series was funded by
The Sears-Roebuck Foundation.

ISBN 0-201-19111-8
ABCDEFGHIJ-AL-798765

To my son, Bradford,
whose almost magical development
has been a constant source
of delight to me.

Editor's Foreword

These are exciting and challenging times in American education. Personnel in local school districts, intermediate education agencies, state education agencies, and teacher education institutions are cooperating as never before to improve the quality of education for children, high school youth, and college students. Bringing Individually Guided Education, a new approach in education, to an ever increasing number of students provides the focus for many of these cooperative efforts. This Leadership Series in Individually Guided Education is designed to aid teacher educators and other educational leaders in their improvement efforts. It comprises ten sets of printed material and correlated films and filmstrips. The materials have been developed for use both in credit courses conducted on college campuses or in local schools and in noncredit staff development programs carried out in the local schools.

The set of materials for child development and Individually Guided Education comprises this textbook and three sound/color filmstrips: *Piagetian Stages of Cognitive Development*, 16 minutes, *Moral Development*, 16 minutes, and *Language Development*, 16 minutes. An accompanying *Instructor's Guide* by Meinke, Leonard, Utz, Yorke, and Cohen provides aids to instructors for meeting the needs of their students in their particular situations.

The author of this textbook, Glenn E. Tagatz, has undertaken two major scholarly tasks. First, he explains major theories of cognitive development, human learning, moral development, and language development and then contrasts them in terms of what each emphasizes as the determinants of child development. He then indicates the implications of certain theories for Individually Guided Education. Necessarily the implications are based on logical analysis and experience in IGE schools, not on research and development to validate the theory or its applications to Individually Guided Education.

I have enjoyed the cooperative and productive working relationships with this scholar, the film producers, the publisher, and others in developing this comprehensive set of multimedia materials. To assure that the users of this and other sets of materials in the Leadership Series get attractive, high quality, usable materials and also are not presented with conflicting interpretations of IGE in either the books or the visuals, I personally reviewed each book from its first chapter outline, through its several field-tested drafts, and the final manuscript. I did the same for each visual from the initial content outline, through the several drafts of the script, rough cuts, and fine cuts. Many other persons also participated in the production, review, and quality control process.

In this regard I am pleased to recognize the many school personnel, state education agency personnel, professors, and students who participated in field tests and review sessions; the consultants with expertise in the various subject matter fields or in the filmic quality and instructional effectiveness of the visuals; Anthony E. Conte, James M. Lipham, Wesley C. Meierhenry, and William Wiersma for serving on the Project Publications Board; Judith Amacker, William R. Bush, James R. Dumpson, Martin W. Essex, Nancy Evers, Lovelia P. Flournoy, John R. Palmer, Edward C. Pomeroy, Richard A. Rossmiller, B. Othanel Smith, Lorraine Sullivan, and James Swinney for serving on the Project Advisory Committee; Leslie C. Bernal, G. R. Bowers, Eleanor Buehrig, Xavier Del Buono, Lee M. Ellwood, G. W. Ford, Marvin J. Fruth, George Glasrud, James Hixson, Ronald Horn, Terry Jackson, L. Wayne Krula, Max Poole, Kenneth B. Smith, James Stoltenberg, Michael F. Tobin, Philip Vik, James E. Walter, S. Edward Weinswig, and William Wiersma for serving on the Project Steering Committee; and the staff of the IGE Teacher Education Project. Particular recognition is given to the members of minority groups who reviewed the visuals in order to avoid having any unintentional racism or sexism appear in them.

The development of these materials became possible through a grant by The Sears-Roebuck Foundation in 1973 to the IGE Teacher Education Project at The University of Wisconsin—Madison. The authors, editor, and others associated with the Project receive no royalties from the sale of these materials. However, the royalties that accrue will be returned to The University of Wisconsin—Madison to support continuing research, development, and implementation activities related to Individually Guided Education.

Herbert J. Klausmeier
Series Editor and Director
IGE Teacher Education Project
The University of Wisconsin—Madison

Preface

This book relates knowledge about child development to Individually Guided Education (IGE). Effort has been made to portray the theories of development as well as IGE practices accurately. There are, however, instances where the amalgamation required the interpretation of one or the other, and here the author may have taken some liberties. I hope that the reader will understand the logic involved. The liberties taken have as their purpose the improvement of educational practices for children. If they produce discourse, the end result should be a better educational climate for children, a purpose the author shares with each reader.

Throughout the book reference is made to a schism which is evident concerning the way different groups of people perceive the nature of humans. Partial validity is found in the empirical research of each of these groups. This volume bridges the gap between what are herein called environmentalists and predeterminists as well as between those theorists who hold to a deterministic philosophy and those who hold to an indeterministic philosophy. It is important for us who teach to periodically reexamine these debates, because such a reexamination allows us to acquire new appreciation of the complexity of human beings and the education process to which they are exposed.

Lastly, the book is an *idea* book as opposed to a cookbook, that is, it cannot be used as a prescriptive formula for dealing with individual children. The ideas are presented as objectives at the beginning of each chapter. Suggested further readings are annotated at the end of each chapter for the student who wants to explore some of the ideas in greater depth. There also are references that provide basic background information into which the book is set. It is my sincere hope that each of you who reads this book will find pleasure and value in exploring the ideas as I have.

I wish to thank the following graduate students who gave help and inspiration during the preparation of this book: Claudia Crawn, Jeff Crisco, Dick Henry, George Hickman, Kee Miner, Helen Swain, Stephan Tchividjian, and Chaille and Rich Walsh. Special appreciation is expressed to Kathy Roblee whose constant help and encouragement made the completion of this book possible.

To my wife, Jan, and my son, Brad, go my thanks for their understanding and support during the hours that were necessary for the book's completion.

Marquette University   G.E.T.
January 1976

Contents

1
Perspectives of Humankind

Objectives

Upon completion of this chapter, the reader should be able:

- To distinguish between and synthesize the various concepts involved in the deterministic and indeterministic approaches to human development.

- To differentiate among the various positions of the free will controversy, analyzing the legitimacy of each.

- To understand the differences among psychoanalytic, cognitive, and learning theories of human development.

- To identify and differentiate among the theories with respect to the following developmental issues:
  a) Nature versus Nurture
  b) Continuity versus Discontinuity
  c) Independence versus Interdependence
  d) Motivation
  e) Learning

- To recognize the educational implications of an interactional approach to development.

*You shall be free indeed when your days are not without
a care nor your nights without a want and a grief,
    But rather when these things girdle your life and yet you
rise above them naked and unbound.*

Kahlil Gibran*

PHILOSOPHICAL PERSPECTIVES

Are we, as humans, computers enacting a script to which we have
been genetically and experientially programmed; or are we free, active, and autonomous agents with the potential to determine our
own future? Is our behavior governed by natural laws and predictable
from antecedent events; or is it a function of individual volition? Are
we the product of evolution, the embodiment of past events which
have caused us to become different in response to our circumstances;
or are we the tailors of our own vestments and the architects of our
own destiny?

Human nature, a traditional topic of philosophical speculation,
has recently acquired psychological attention as well. Philosophers
have approached this issue from two basic points of view, with many
compromises in between. One group of philosophers views humans
as pawns of a predetermined fate, while another group sees humans
as autonomous and self-determined agents. The first view is deterministic; the second is indeterministic and currently characterized
by the existential viewpoint.

These two orientations can be traced to the beginnings of recorded history. Anthropological studies indicate that early cave
dwellers felt a sense of helplessness resulting, apparently, from the
belief that their lives were governed by natural elements and external
environmental forces. Accordingly, they worshiped powerful natural
forces in an attempt to appease them and created elaborate mythol-
ogies to explain what they could not understand. Anthropological
findings further indicate that cave dwellers tried to achieve symbolic
control of the future by drawing on cave walls the animals they hoped
to kill in future hunts. Such activities represent primitive instances
of human speculation concerning the nature of being. They reflect

---

* Reprinted from *The prophet,* by Kahlil Gibran, with the permission of
the publisher, Alfred A. Knopf, Inc. Copyright 1923 by Kahlil Gibran;
renewal copyright 1951 by Administrators C.T.A. of Kahlil Gibran Estate,
and Mary G. Gibran.

contradictory concepts of humans as both controlled and controlling beings.

Determinism

Determinism is the philosophical position which holds that all occurrences in the universe are ordered and follow from antecedent conditions. Proponents of this position state that all events are determined by previous events. Deterministic doctrine is used as a source of description and explanation by philosophers and scientists alike to explain both the physical characteristics of the universe and the behavioral characteristics of humans. Because of these varied applications, the definition of determinism requires clarification.

The primary theme of determinism is that humans lack control over events. According to this theory, all events are predetermined and occur in a predictable manner. Examples of deterministic belief abound in ancient literature: Oedipus was fated to kill his father and marry his mother. This was foreseen by a prophet and all precautions taken to prevent its occurrence were to no avail. Similarly, in literature the real battle for the city of Troy was fought on Mount Olympus. The gods used Greeks and Trojans as puppets through whom they worked out their celestial squabbles. The Calvinist doctrine of predeterminism exemplifies a religious application of the phenomenon. To the Calvinist, each person is born already destined for salvation or damnation and can do nothing consciously in life to change this. Clearly, early writings and religious doctrines reflected the times during which they occurred: Human destiny was not in human control, but seemed to be in the grip of supernatural forces. Early people stubbornly sought some assurance that surrounding events did not occur by chance—even they had a primitive knowledge of cause and effect.

An assumption underlying deterministic perspectives is that the universe is an ordered place where all events follow natural laws. The philosophical view of determinism emphasizes fatalism, or lack of choice, whereas the scientific view emphasizes the cause and effect relationship between events. In extending this latter view, Schlick (1949) reported that when scientists use the term determinism, they are asserting the possibility of prediction. That is the extent to which scientists know that the occurrence of a particular event is consistently followed by a subsequent event dictates the degree of certainty with which they can predict the latter from the occurrence of the former.

The influence of determinism on the behavioral sciences is evident in the statement that human behavior is restricted by natural laws. Individuals who study behavior use a process of observing, measuring, and predicting behavior. Psychologists who hold a deterministic position focus on the relationship they find between their observations and their successful predictions. They believe that a cause must come before its effect, so they often probe an individual's past in searching for the cause of that individual's present behavior. To the deterministic scientist, humans not only exist in a lawful and completely determined universe, but they are determined parts of that universe. Humans are the result of their genetic heritage and the way this heritage is acted upon by prenatal and postnatal circumstances. Psychologists adhering to the deterministic position hold that an individual's behavior is completely shaped or determined by the influences that act upon that individual. Presented with total knowledge of the previous history of an individual, they believe science could predict exactly how that individual would act.

Indeterminism

Indeterminism is a philosophical position which takes exception to the cause-effect position of determinism. It assumes that novelty, freedom, or chance characterize the relation of events as well as, if not more than, cause and effect. Indeterminism generally refers to a probabilistic model of human or physical behavior in which variation from causal-effect relationships is acknowledged. That is, in any circumstance, probabilistic variation will occur; and it therefore would be impossible to predict with 100 percent certainty any single occurrence no matter how much one knows about the past history and experience of the organism. Indeterminism assumes that new experience holds to a probabilistic model where the organism makes responses to circumstances without complete predictability from prior events. Because variability exists, a human's actions are not completely caused. Human beings can and do make choices concerning their behavior.

Indeterminism contains the basic assumptions of the currently popular philosophy of existentialism which perhaps best exemplifies this position. Existentialism (Hilgard and Atkinson 1967) is a philosophical viewpoint which emphasizes "that man is not a ready-made machine, but rather that he has the freedom to make vital choices and to assume responsibility for his own existence. It emphasizes subjective experience as a sufficient criterion of truth." Existentialists find the universe to be chaotic and unordered. Plagues, wars, and all other inhumanities follow no predictable, logical plan. This realization, states the existentialist, is behind the alienation and purposelessness which is evident in modern society. Faced with this unordered universe, existentialists can save themselves from utter despair only by imposing a personal order. They prescribe this order by active choice. The existentialist perceives freedom in personal thoughts and actions and assumes the responsibilities which accompany this freedom of choice.

Presently, one of the best known existentialists is Jean Paul Sartre. To Sartre (1962) persons' existence precedes their essence. This means that persons are not determined by any previously given nature; rather they make their own nature. Therefore, they are free in the sense of not being predetermined. Sartre describes persons as recognizing freedom when they recognize the nothingness in their hearts. This realization compels them to make themselves into something. To Sartre persons get their essence by creating it themselves through making choices and through engaging or committing themselves. Until they consciously give meaning and purpose to their own lives through their choices, and accept the responsibilities this entails, persons merely exist.

Martin Heidegger (1962) arrived at existentialism in a way similar to Sartre. He distinguished between life and existence, existence being of one's own making. Everyone has a life, but individuals create their own existence. Life has various degrees—good or bad, long or short—but existence has no degrees. Heidegger is renowned for his 'being-in-the-world' concept, which implies a world of interaction. To Heidegger, the word 'being' involves a certain amount of anguish as a result of interaction. Humans cannot exist outside the world, yet their existence in the world is curtailed by their dependence on the reality which surrounds them. In contrast to Sartre's emphasis on the importance of responsibility in making choices, Heidegger emphasizes the gloomy aspects of freedom. To Heidegger, free persons are engaged in a constant struggle to accept their dependence on the world, while recognizing their individual freedom and the limitations of their being.

In contrast to Heidegger and Sartre are existentialists such as Marcel (1951), Buber (1947), and Maurice Merleau-Ponty (1962), who view humans not only as free but as able to fulfill their freedom through communion with others. Communion with others holds similar meaning to all three, and is exemplified by Buber's I-Thou relationship. I-Thou is not a nothingness or an anguish. Rather, it is a fulfillment of humans in which their being is freed through communication with others. It is in contrast with the I-It relationship in which a person interacts with others as objects, i.e., without the communication of being. To Buber and other existentialists like him, Sartre and Heidegger are examples of unfulfilled freedom, for they do not transcend their dependent nature by establishing I-Thou communication.

Thus existentialism is a broad school of philosophical thought which reflects the indeterminant nature of humans. Such indeterminance affords humans the opportunity for choice and change. The existentialists, emphasizing the indeterminant nature of behavior, would say that choice and change are the manifestations of human freedom. Determinists would likely say that choice and change are illusions. What humans perceive as choice and change are merely the functions of antecedent events. Thus determinists deny that humans have freedom. What then are the alternatives to an acceptance or rejection of freedom? What are the alternatives implicit for causality and prediction?

Determinism versus Freedom

The ancient Greeks attempted to rationalize the seeming contradiction between determinism and freedom by espousing a theory of duality. A human was viewed as being composed of two parts: the body and the soul. Knowledge and freedom were attributed to the soul, which was imprisoned by the pleasure-seeking propensities of the body. By divorcing oneself from the physical distractions of everyday life, one gained freedom of nature. Hence Socrates, in defense of the human right to knowledge and independence, exercised freedom and actively chose death by suicide rather than a life of imposed silence.

On the contemporary scene, D'Angelo (1968) delineates four possible positions pertinent to the determinism versus freedom controversy:

1. Freedom is false and determinism is true.
2. Freedom is true and determinism is false.
3. Both determinism and freedom are true.
4. Both determinism and freedom are false.

This fourth and last position is discounted at the outset. It seems that rational arguments cannot be made for it. This then leaves three positions to be examined.

The position that freedom is false and determinism is true has a certain appeal to scientifically oriented generations. It has been repeatedly demonstrated in the physical sciences that the universe is subject to natural laws. Why then should this not be true of human behavior? A particular individual is the product of inherited and experientially determined characteristics—and nothing more. Such hardline determinism implies that one then is not responsible for one's actions. Is this the reason for a moratorium on capital punishment? Is this the reason for rehabilitation replacing penal incarceration? The concept of moral responsibility becomes a mere intellectual exercise. The individual is not responsible. Transgressions are the fault of the antecedent events in life or genetic inheritance.

The position that freedom is true and determinism is false has a strong appeal for many people. Part of this appeal results from the fact that the position places humans above inanimate objects and above other forms of animal life. It makes humans supreme. Human beings are the makers of their own destinies: They have the ability to choose and are responsible for their actions. Thus this position conforms with the popularly held notion of human existence. Rehabilitation, penal incarceration, or execution can be justified according to this position also. However, it is not human beings' predetermined nature that dictates what society should do. Rather, it is persons as members of society that choose among alternatives, making the choice on the basis of what they have first made of themselves in their struggle for being. Those that choose become responsible for their choice.

The position that both freedom and determinism are true is a possibility which many people overlook. Philosophers who recognize that an act can be both free and determined have been termed soft determinists. The soft determinist holds that certain errors are responsible for the belief that determinism and freedom are mutually exclusive. These errors lie in the definitions of freedom and determinism. Soft determinists propose that determinism should not be equated with fatalism, nor freedom with complete freedom of choice. Soft determinists believe that determinism and freedom can both be components of humans. James (1884), an early American philosopher, felt that the conflict between freedom and determinism could not be resolved since both may be true.

For behavioral scientists the soft determinist view is probably the most germane of the three alternatives. Genetic determinism in the area of physical characteristics cannot be denied. Freedom in the utilization of ideas in ways not found in one's environment is also undeniable. Einstein, Edison, and Marconi provide striking evidence that some persons can go beyond what existed in their antecedent environment. Scientific theory is thus most compatible with a soft deterministic philosophy.

DEVELOPMENTAL PERSPECTIVES

Developmental Theories Identified

Arising from the philosophical considerations of human nature, one would expect parallel systems of development, i.e., one system emphasizing human freedom only, one emphasizing both freedom and determinism, and one emphasizing determinism only. This pattern is somewhat evident within the broad continuum of psychological theory where behaviorism as characterized by Skinner (1971) is largely deterministic, humanism as characterized by Victor Frankl (1972) accents the indeterminant or existential nature of man, and cognitive psychologists such as Piaget (1963) characterize the soft deterministic position.

Considering the controversial nature of the determinism-freedom issue, it is not surprising to discover that it has also infiltrated the realm of developmental psychology. Developmental psychology, which deals with the acquisition over time of psychomotor, affective, and cognitive behaviors by the human organism, also mirrors this philosophical continuum in the theoretical orientation of its scientists. The orientations of psychologists tend toward behaviorism or humanism depending on their emphasis on either the act or the actor.

Due to the fact that developmental psychology is a science and as such assumes a certain amount of order and causality in behavior, purely existential developmental psychologists do not exist. No matter how humanistic their personal philosophies might be, they still assume some degree of cause and effect in the universe in general and in the development of human behavior in particular. Similarly, no matter how deterministic their personal philosophy might be, they still assume that some degree of novelty, freedom, *or* chance enters into the development of an organism. All developmental psychologists accept all the facts, only their interpretations differ. Accordingly, while all developmental psychologists fall near the center of the hard determinism-soft determinism-freedom continuum, their exact position along this continuum is determined by their interpretation of the facts. For example, in affective development (Chapter 5) Maslow's need theory would fall on the freedom side of soft determinism because metaneeds arise from the unique variation in each man's development. Likewise in affective development, Bandura and Walters's social learning theory would fall on the deterministic side of soft determinism because conditioning and modeling are explanations of environmentally induced change, and emphasize the predictable aspects of human development.

While the hard determinism-soft determinism-freedom continuum provides one philosophical dimension upon which developmental theories can be logically differentiated, current textbook authors such as Mussen, Conger, and Kagan (1969) prefer to categorize developmental theories into learning theory, psychoanalytic theory, and cognitive theory. Examples of learning theories of development are the cumulative learning theories of Gagne and Skinner (Chapter 3).

Examples of cognitive theories of development are the theories of Piaget and Bruner (Chapter 3). An example of a psychoanalytically oriented theory is Erikson's psychosocial theory (Chapter 5). These categories also provide a means of logically differentiating the various developmental theories. However, the differentiation is more complex and is made on the basis of a number of developmental issues in addition to the determinism-freedom issue.

ISSUES IN DEVELOPMENT

Nature-Nurture Issue

One of the major issues differentiating among learning theorists, psychoanalytic theorists, and cognitive theorists is the nature-nurture issue. This issue refers to a controversy among theorists as to whether development is primarily influenced by heredity (nature) or environment (nurture). As in the determinism-freedom issue, the extremes of the nature-nurture continuum are not represented in the area of developmental psychology. All theorists agree that both heredity and environment are involved in the developmental process. Rather, the major difference among developmental theorists arises from the question: To what extent does heredity influence development and to what extent does environment influence development? Learning theorists such as Skinner and Gagne favor the environmental side of the continuum (nurture) and consequently may be called environmentalists. Cognitive theorists such as Piaget and Bruner and psychoanalytic theorists such as Erikson fall on the hereditary side of the continuum (nature) for they postulate predetermined stages of development. These theorists consequently may be called predeterminists.

Environmentalists

The environmentalist maximizes the influence of the child's internal and external environment, and minimizes that of innate, inherited tendencies, and structures. The external environment includes all stimuli reaching the senses of the individual: sight, taste, touch, sound, smell. Even the validity of measuring stimuli to and response from the so-called sixth sense is being investigated in ESP (extrasensory perception) research. Internal environment includes physiological stimuli and reactions within the body, such as fear or attention level.

Essentially *tabulae rasae* or blank slates at birth, children are bombarded by these internal and external stimuli which make impressions on them directing and determining the outcome of their

Some similarities can be attributed to heredity (physical characteristics of twins), and other characteristics can be attributed to environment (separate interests).

development. Rewarding some of the acquisitions and punishing others cause certain behaviors to be encouraged and retained and others to be discouraged and eliminated. Unique environmental conditions act upon the malleable children to direct the course of their development.

A name which has become almost synonymous with the environmental position in recent years is B. F. Skinner, a learning theorist. In his book *Beyond Freedom and Dignity,* Skinner (1971) articulates the ways in which environmental control can and should be used to raise human developmental level. Since behavior is believed to be contingent upon environmental stimulation and reinforcement, the environment can be manipulated to promote the most efficient human development in the least possible time.

Predeterminists

The predeterminist emphasizes innate factors which determine and regulate the direction of human development. The dinosaur of predeterministic doctrines was preformationism, a discipline now universally recognized as fallacious. The preformationist viewed the human fetus as a "little man" possessing all the "seeds" of the qualities which the child would exhibit later in life. For example, a preformationist would state that the caterpillar literally carried within itself a miniature butterfly which became larger inside the cocoon. The structures of the caterpillar did not metamorphasize into the structures of the butterfly. All human characteristics, the preformationist believed, existed at conception and unfolded sequentially on a prearranged schedule. The last of the great preformationist debates concerned whether this "little man" was present in the egg of the female or the sperm of the male.

With the advent of sophisticated microscopes and the sciences of embryology and genetics, preformationism was retired to the history books, and replaced by predeterminism. The predeterminists believe that an individual possesses an innate dimension of development which increases at a set pace to a predetermined level. As an example, this theory holds that intelligence is inherited genetically and unfolds automatically with anatomical maturation until it reaches preestablished boundaries. This theory gave rise to the intelligence quotient, or IQ test. If intelligence is a fixed, inherited quality, predeterminists stated, then it can be measured, compared, and used to predict. This process would apply equally to all human development, physical and psychological as well.

Predeterminism carried to an extreme would see value in eugenics, the study of the selective breeding of human beings. If limits to development are inherited genetically, then only the most intelligent and healthiest humans should be allowed to reproduce in the interest of the improvement of the species. This issue, obviously, raises serious moral questions.

Originally the nature-nurture controversy represented diametrically opposed viewpoints. The predeterminists maintained that nature or genetic endowment was the overriding factor. The environmentalists completely rejected that position. How much of human behavior is the result of nature and how much the result of nurture? The issue is still very much alive today, and it has a marked impact on developmental theory and on educational practice.

Examples of the nature-nurture controversy are much in evidence in the literature on human development. Researchers, such as Newman, Freeman, and Holzinger (1937), holding the position that intelligence is an innate characteristic, usually support their opinion with the findings obtained from studies of twins. Such studies have revealed a high correlation between intelligence test scores of identical twins when they are raised apart in different environments.

Evidence is also available to support the opposing view, that intelligence is the product of an individual's environment. Studies such as those reported by Bayley (1970) have indicated that both social and academic factors can alter intelligence test scores. Factors such as educational opportunity, economic status, education of parents, and social class have been found to affect test scores on standardized tests. The question can be raised, however, as to whether, for example, socioeconomic level is the product of experiential factors or whether innate factors cause changes in socioeconomic level of subsequent generations.

Similarly, studies have been done in the affective and psychomotor domains of human behavior with results which also support both positions. The emerging consensus seems to be that the interaction of the two factors is the most defensible position.

Continuity versus Discontinuity

Another issue differentiating among learning theorists, psychoanalytic theorists, and cognitive theorists is the continuity-discontinuity issue. This issue refers to a controversy among theorists as to whether development occurs primarily in a continuous progression or whether it occurs in a series of stages.

According to some cognitive and psychoanalytic theorists, development is dominated by the emergence of innately regulated mechanisms leading to discontinuity in behavior. Such modifications imply a metamorphosis, that is, humans are something different than they were at a previous developmental stage. Discontinuity in development suggests that the acquisition of behaviors depends upon the biologically induced stage at which the individual is operating. For example, in cognitive development, cognitive stage theorists represent the discontinuity position. For cognitive stage theorists, information processing functions differently at different stages, therefore learning is different at each stage. Thus, what or how individuals learn at age 40 is qualitatively different from what or how they learned at age two. When a stage is completed, and no sooner, individuals progress to the next stage. Each stage represents a new mode of operation previously not available to the learner. These stages are predetermined and invariant, that is, each individual goes through the stages in the same order as every other individual. No one skips any stages.

According to learning theorists, development is continuous and unvarying except in the richness of the experiences to which an individual is subjected. This position is exemplified in cognitive development by cumulative learning theorists. Cumulative learning theorists believe that cognitive associations about reality are gradually accumulated. In a continuous progression, each new bit of information is added to what has been previously learned. Learning accrues. Such continuity implies that what and/or how an individual learns at age 40 is qualitatively present and supported by what was learned at age two.

The continuity-discontinuity issue has significant implications for education. If continuity is true, any curricular material may be introduced in some appropriate form at any time in the development of the learner. If discontinuity is true, certain educational experiences should be postponed until the learner has reached a developmental stage which is consonant with the material to be learned. If discontinuity is true, still another question emerges: Can the developmental stages be accelerated through experience? As you encounter subsequent chapters of this book, you will observe the continuity versus discontinuity issue as it has been resolved by the three categories of developmental theorists. For our present purpose it suffices to say that educators await a definitive answer to this issue while using the best empirical data available in the educative processes for which they have responsibility.

Independence versus Interdependence

Another issue which distinguishes among learning theorists, psychoanalytic theorists, and cognitive theorists concerns whether development within the cognitive, affective, and psychomotor domains is interrelated or independent. Does development in each area reach approximately the same level before the individual progresses on to higher developmental levels? What occurs within each area with respect to the content of different subject areas? If cognitive, affective, and psychomotor behaviors are independent, then each should exhibit separate development. In other words, an individual could be slow in psychomotor development, average in affective development, and above average in cognitive development. Carrying this independence of development even further, within the cognitive domain an individual could think abstractly in mathematics but not in social science, depending on the difference in experience and practice the individual obtained in each.

With regard to different areas of development, theorists appear to agree that an individual's cognitive, affective, and psychomotor development can be at different levels at the same time. An individual may be slow in psychomotor development, average in affective development, and above average in cognitive development. However, within the various areas of development a controversy about independence does exist. For example, in the cognitive domain learning theorists assert that an individual may be capable of thinking abstractly in mathematics while not yet being able to think abstractly in social studies, dependent on the individual's previous experiences in these subjects. This is an independent approach in which gradual quantitative change occurs within areas. The opposing position represented by some of the cognitive theorists is that the ability to think abstractly develops at the same time in all cognitive areas. This controversy remains a theoretical issue not only in the area of cognitive development but also in the affective and psychomotor areas. The position of various theorists in this controversy will become more evident in subsequent chapters.

Motivation

Another issue in development which differentiates among learning theorists, psychoanalytic theorists, and cognitive theorists concerns the nature of motivation. Do humans merely react in response to internal and external stimuli which impinge upon them causing disequilibrium, or do they seek disequilibrium, acting upon their environment to change it?

Learning theorists such as Skinner state that the primary needs for food, water, and physical comfort are the foundation upon which learned needs are based. Because of the drive reduction which occurs when these needs are met, secondary objects such as the mother who provides food and comfort, and later, objects like money which can be used to secure food and so forth, take on the reinforcing qualities of the needed nurturants. According to these theorists an organism seeks homeostasis, that is, an equilibrium with the environment.

In contrast, some cognitive theorists such as Piaget, and some psychoanalytic theorists such as Erikson, believe that the human organism seeks more than the reduction of physiologically based needs. Piaget states that all organisms seek to organize their environment (Chapter 3). Erikson states that humans seek goals such as independence and self-identity (Chapter 5). Such stimulation theorists emphasize the curiosity, activity, and satisfaction demonstrated by the human organism as it acquires mastery of its environment. Satisfaction in task performance is believed to be the goal and the end product of human activity. Stimulation theorists, then, emphasize the active nature of the human organism and attribute to it curiosity and a desire for environmental control.

Learning

The final issue to be considered in this chapter which differentiates among learning theorists, psychoanalytic theorists, and cognitive theorists concerns the nature of learning. Most psychologists would accept as a definition of learning something like the following: Learning is a process through which behavior is changed as a result of experience. This definition has different meanings for psychologists depending upon the basic theoretical position of the individual. Two diverse positions have emerged. One is an associationist position and the other is a field theory position.

Associative learning theorists as opposed to cognitive and psychoanalytic theorists ascribe to an associationist theory of learning. Such a theory emphasizes the associations that are made between stimuli and the resultant responses. It is this emphasis on association which gives the name to the position. If the right stimulus is presented, or the appropriate response reinforced, behavior is changed as a result of the association. The classical conditioning paradigm of Pavlov, the instrumental conditioning paradigm of Skinner, and the hierarchical paradigm of Gagne, explained in Chapter 3, are associationist positions. The position is mechanistic and reductive, i.e., human behavior can be reduced to the antecedent conditions of human experience. For these theorists, cognitive, affective, and psychomotor behavior can all be explained by this principle. The totality of the human organism's being is no more or less than the sum of the mechanistic associations that have come as antecedent conditions, either genetically or experientially.

Cognitive theorists ascribe to a field theory of learning. To field theorists, antecedent events may be significant in determining a human's existence, but they do not provide a complete explanation. Humans themselves through their powers of cognition, are capable of interpreting their physical and social world. Thus, the totality of being is more than the sum of mechanistic associations. Field theorists place emphasis on the individual's perception of experience and the meaning that the learner gives to experience. All experience then is unique to the individual because of personal unique perception.

EDUCATIONAL PERSPECTIVE

Thus far in this chapter, development has been viewed from both a philosophical and a theoretical perspective. Such perspectives are concerned primarily with explaining why and how development occurs. In contrast to these perspectives there is an educational perspective which is primarily concerned with detecting what types of learning experiences and learning environments will optimize the developmental potential of humankind. Such a perspective differs from both a philosophical and a theoretical perspective in that it is more concerned with the facts obtained through research, and less concerned with explaining why such facts were obtained. An educational perspective on development must accept all the significant findings, no matter what their philosophical or theoretical implications.

The educator is able to accept such a paradoxical position concerning human development by taking an eclectic, soft determinist position which is herein termed interactionism. Interactionism accepts the fact that behavior is at times predictable and at times unpredictable. The interactionist is in the middle of the hard determinism-soft determinism-freedom continuum, viewing humans as both active and reactive beings. To the interactionist, individuals are and individuals become according to the forces that act upon them, including what they choose or will for themselves. Thus the teacher who conscientiously plans a series of lessons can understand and capitalize on student deviations from this lesson plan.

With respect to the nature-nurture issue, the interactionist does not become concerned about the extent to which either nature or nurture affects development. Rather, the interactionist accepts the fact that both nature and nurture interact in the process of development, and strives to provide optimal developmental conditions in all respects. Consequently, the interactionist recognizes good prenatal care, parental education, Head Start, "Sesame Street," and so forth as efforts to modify the experiential base with which the developing child interacts.

With respect to the continuity-discontinuity issue, interactionism when defined as the belief that an organism both reacts to its environment and acts upon its environment, accepts either side of the issue. Interactionists can believe in continuity, discontinuity, or both without contradicting their position. Generally, interactionists take the pragmatic position of advocating whatever educational practices work in fostering development.

With respect to the independence-interdependence issue, the interactionist favors a mild interdependent position because each individual *in that individual's entirety* is actively involved in the developmental process. Thus the interactionist would state that in the cognitive domain, an individual's ability to think abstractly in mathematics may or may not be accomplished at the same time as an individual's ability to think abstractly in social studies, but that each potentially influences the other. This position of mild interdependence is based on the fact that all an individual's cognitive experiences interact with the individual's previous cognitive knowledge and affect each bit of that knowledge in some way. Notably, the interactionist need not adhere to a strict interdependent position in which cognitive development reaches the same level at the same time within all cognitive areas, but a mild interdependence within developmental areas is dictated by the fact that the entire human organism plays an active part in the interactive developmental process.

With respect to motivation, the interactionist who views humans as active in their own development favors the theoretical belief that humans seek stimulation and disequilibrium in order to acquire control over their environment. This does not disavow that humans may also seek equilibrium in certain instances or even discount the possibility that the human organism learns that in order to satisfy needs it must actively place itself in an unbalanced position to obtain control over its environment. Rather, this position is a mild stimulation position which allows the interactionist to use either or both explanations of motivation to foster a desire to learn in individual students.

Finally, with respect to how learning occurs, the interactionist believes that both the associationist explanation of how environment affects learning and the field theory explanation of how an individual's perception affects learning are pertinent for educational practice. Associationism describes how environment affects human learning and consequently conforms to the interactive view of a human as a reactive being. Field theory describes how an individual's unique perception affects learning, and consequently conforms to the interactive view of a human as an active being. Through utilizing these two theoretical approaches to learning, the interactionist is able to promote all types of development in students, from simple labeling of letters to complex, abstract problem-solving.

In conclusion, human development may be viewed from a philosophical, theoretical, or educational perspective, depending upon what developmental questions one feels are of primary importance. However, no matter what the perspective, it becomes evident that each human life has a complexity which makes the individual an unique entity. Humankind may be free, or may be determined; or may be both free and determined. It may be the product of genetic and experiential factors; and/or it may be the product of factors of self-fulfillment. Whatever your resolution of what the nature of humankind really is, it is obvious that *Homo sapiens* demonstrates an involved and intricate character which is unmatched by any other species on the face of the earth and that each individual requires an educational experience which will allow that individual to realize full potential.

SUGGESTED READINGS FOR CHAPTER 1

Skinner, B. F. 1971. *Beyond freedom and dignity.* New York: Knopf.

Skinner argues that our traditional concepts of freedom and dignity must be revised. He says "a technology of behavior comparable in power and precision to physical and biological technology" is needed, thus challenging the philosophical position of indeterminism described in this chapter.

Jensen, A. 1971. The differences are real. *Psychology Today* (December).

In his article, Jensen questions the doctrine of racial genetic equality. He proposes that the average differences of blacks and whites in their performance on IQ tests may be attributed to heredity, thus advocating the predeterministic approach to development described in this chapter.

D'Angelo, E. 1968. *The problem of freedom and determinism.* Columbia, Mo.: University of Missouri Press.

In order to help differentiate among various positions of the free will controversy this analysis of indeterminism, soft determinism, and hard determinism will help clarify whether freedom is or is not compatible with determinism.

REFERENCES

Ausubel, D. P. 1958. *Theories and problems of child development.* New York: Grune and Stratton.

Bayley, N. 1970. Development of mental abilities. In P. H. Mussen (ed.), *Carmichael's manual of child psychology.* Vol. 1. (3rd ed.) New York: Wiley.

Buber, M. 1947. *Between man and man.* London: Kegan Paul.

Coleman, J. C. 1969. *Psychology and effective behavior.* Glenview, Ill.: Scott Foresman.

D'Angelo, E. 1968. *The problem of freedom and determinism.* Columbia, Mo.: University of Missouri Press.

Frankl, V. 1972. *Man's search for meaning: an introduction to logotherapy.* New York: Simon & Schuster.

Gesell, A. 1933. Maturation and the patterning of behavior. In C. A. Murchinson (ed.), *A handbook of child psychology.* Worcester, Mass.: Clark University Press.

Gibran, K. 1923. *The prophet.* New York: Knopf.

Heidegger, M. 1962. *Being and time*. London: SCM Press.

Hilgard, E. R., and R. C. Atkinson 1967. *Introduction to psychology*. (4th ed.) New York: Harcourt.

James, W. 1884. The dilemma of determinism. *The Unitarian Review* (September).

Leaky, A. M. 1935. Nature-nurture and intelligence. *Genetic Psychological Monograph* 17: 235–308.

Lorge, I. 1945. Schooling makes a difference. *Teachers College Record* 46: 483–492.

Marcel, G. 1951. *The mystery of being*. Vol. 2. Chicago: Henry Regnery.

Merleau-Ponty, M. 1962. *Phenomenology of perception*. New York: Humanities Press.

Newman, H. H., F. N. Freeman, and K. J. Holzinger 1937. *Twins: a study of heredity and environment*. Chicago: University of Chicago Press.

Piaget, J. 1962. *The origins of intelligence in children*. New York: Norton.

Sartre, J. P. 1962. *Sketch for a theory of the emotions*. London: Methuen.

Schlick, M. 1949. Causality in everyday life and in recent science. In H. Feigel and W. Sellars (eds.), *Readings in philosophical analysis*. New York: Appleton-Century-Crofts.

Shockley, W. 1972. A debate challenge: Geneticity is 80% for white identical twins' IQs. *Phi Delta Kappan* 53: 415–419.

Skinner, B. F. 1971. *Beyond freedom and dignity*. New York: Knopf.

Wheeler, L. R. 1942. A comparative study of the intelligence of East Tennessee mountain children. *Journal of Educational Psychology* 33: 321–334.

2

Individually Guided Education as a Facilitative Environment

Objectives

Upon completion of this chapter, the reader should be able:

- To identify and distinguish among the cognitive, affective, and psychomotor domains of human behavior.
- To demonstrate an understanding of the components of Individually Guided Education.
- To analyze the ways that the model of instructional programming for the individual student:
  a) Is consonant with developmental theory.
  b) Provides for commonalities in children's development.
  c) Provides for individual differences in children's development.
- To articulate ways in which Individually Guided Education fosters development in the cognitive, affective and psychomotor domains of human behavior.
- To describe the way in which Individually Guided Education reflects societal values and humans as interactive agents with their environments.

If a man does not keep pace
with his companions, perhaps it is because
he hears a different drummer.
Let him step to the music which he hears,
however measured or far away.

Henry David Thoreau

INDIVIDUAL DIFFERENCES AND THE NEED FOR AN EDUCATIONAL SYSTEM TO COMPLEMENT THEM

It was 8 o'clock and school was about to begin. In Room 200 at Washington Elementary School, Miss Peterson was placing the day's arithmetic assignment on the chalkboard. In the Instructional Materials Center at Lincoln Elementary School on the other side of town, Miss Johnson and other teachers were placing individualized learning materials on each of their students' desks, except those of Sue and Jim, for whom a clear desk in the morning meant assurance that they wouldn't be under too much pressure to learn a particular amount of material that day. The school bells rang. The students in Miss Peterson's room filed through the door and took their seats in the rows of precisely arranged desks. The students in Miss Johnson's unit scattered upon entering the room, some going to their desks to see what their teachers had just placed there, some to the book nook in the corner, some to watch the fish eat breakfast, some to finish yesterday's art project, some to check the weather station, and still others to talk with Miss Johnson about assignments on which they were working.

The difference between these two environments is obvious. Miss Peterson's class is typical of the traditional school in which all children are taught in the same manner. Miss Johnson's unit is typical of Individually Guided Education (IGE) schools in which instructional programming for the individual student is practiced. In Miss Johnson's unit each child is taught in a manner and setting planned to meet that child's individual strengths, weaknesses and learning style.

The IGE school, also called the multiunit school, is one which provides instructional programming for the individual student. Individually guided education (Klausmeier 1975) was formulated on the premise that instruction should be adapted to meet the needs of children, each of whom is unique. The concept of individuality is not new in the study of human development. Wilhelm Wundt, founder of the first psychological laboratory in 1879, studied differences in human reaction time in his laboratory. Also, the nature-nurture controversy was generated and continues because of individual differences. The existence of individual differences is widely accepted by developmental theorists; yet, individual differences in development are overlooked in a wide variety of instances by educators. In contrast, IGE is an alternative form of schooling designed to provide for individual differences in human development. The organizational administrative arrangement of an IGE school is designated multiunit and provides the means by which the other components of IGE are introduced into the school.

The average child is a mathematical phenomenon rather than an actual child. School classrooms are filled with students who are not average. Deviations in physical development are probably the most obvious differences between the hypothetical, average child and the real, classroom child. However, the differences in intellectual and emotional development quickly become apparent after observing students and working with them in school activities.

The phenomenon of the average child has resulted from psychologists attempting to discover lawful regularities in development and behavior. One of the most common research methods used in attempting to discover similarities among children is the study of large groups of subjects. Nomothetic research is the term applied to research using large groups of subjects. When large groups are studied for purposes of discovering similarities among them, a particular type of nomothetic research, termed normative research, is used to describe the study.

In contrast to nomothetic research is idiographic research which studies one subject in greater detail. When small groups of subjects are studied in detail using idiographic research methods, for purposes of discovering individual differences, a particular type of idiographic research, termed clinical research, is used to describe the study.

While both normative and clinical research are useful to the developmental psychologist and educational practitioner, educators have, too often, overlooked the educational implications derived from clinical research. IGE is a response by educators to the need for an educational system which meets the unique qualities and interests of the individual learner.

In studying individual differences in human development, researchers and theorists often divide development into three areas: (1) the cognitive, which refers to intellectual functioning; (2) the affective, which refers to emotional and social functioning; and (3) the psychomotor, which refers to physical functioning. These three areas of study may be considered an arbitrary division used in the study of human development. These divisions do not alter the fact that humans act and react as whole, integrated beings. The divisions do, however, provide a means of studying different aspects of human behavior and afford the opportunity of observing human individuality.

Cognitive Domain

Cognition is the process of knowing or it is the product of such a process. As a process, the cognitive domain is concerned with the way in which humans come to know about themselves and their surroundings. As a product, the cognitive domain is concerned with the way in which humans have organized and internalized representations of self, surroundings, and ideas. These process and product definitions of the cognitive domain result in two major approaches to the study of cognitive development, a process approach and a structural approach. The process approach emphasizes the ways in which humans come to know themselves and their surroundings such as perceiving, thinking, remembering, evaluating, etc. The structural approach emphasizes the stages in the organization of thought common to every person as progress is made toward maturity. In a practical sense, process and product cannot be separated, and an examination of individual differences in the cognitive domain reveals differences in both process and structure which are influenced by a variety of factors.

Studies by Beard (1961) and Hood (1962) concerning the development of quantitative thinking illustrate these process and product differences in cognition. Using the same structural model of cognitive development which was developed by Piaget (1963) both found that children with high intelligence were more likely to be at an advanced stage of cognitive development than were children who were less intelligent. In addition, based upon data from 125 subjects, Hood reported that prenumber concepts did not usually develop until a child was six to seven years old, and that mental age was of far greater importance in determining conceptual level than was chronological age. Beard reported similar findings and also identified sex-based differences in understanding number concepts. This normative research emphasizes the many factors influencing stage or product attainment.

Using an idiographic research model, Beard studied differences within qualitative thinking at particular stages. He found that children differed to some degree even in the sequence in which they understood concepts. Some subjects could count fluently but were unable to handle simple conservation problems such as recognizing which of two numbers indicated a larger quantity, whereas others who counted poorly were able to complete all the conceptual prob-

Development may be divided into three areas: cognitive, affective, and psychomotor.

lems on the test. This research emphasizes the differences in cognitive processes within a qualitative thinking stage.

These and similar studies indicate vast individual differences in both cognitive processes and cognitive structure among children of the same age. That is, individual children of the same chronological age differ markedly in terms of their levels of cognitive functioning and in terms of the way that they function. These differences may be due to past learning opportunities, sex-based learning opportunities, biological maturation, general intelligence, etc. Why the differences occur is not quite as important as the fact that they do occur. They need to be recognized and given consideration in the entire formal educative process.

Other differences in cognitive functioning have been identified by researchers which differ from those associated with mental ability and such demographic factors as sex, age, and ethnic background. Such differences, which do not fall under the conventional classification of abilities, are referred to as differences in cognitive style. Such differences pertain to the manner of cognition rather than the degree of success or failure in cognition, though certain cognitive styles may lead to more appropriate responses for learners engaged in particular types of tasks.

Cognitive styles are systematic methods of perceiving, processing, remembering, and responding to information characteristic of individuals and maintained by individuals across time and across experience. Messick (1969) summarized some of the research and delineated dimensions of cognitive styles: (1) field independence versus field dependence, (2) scanning, (3) breadth of categorizing, (4) conceptualizing style, (5) cognitive complexity versus simplicity, (6) reflectivity versus impulsivity, (7) leveling versus sharpening, (8) constricted versus flexible control, and (9) tolerance for incongruous or unrealistic experiences. Each of these nine dimensions may be categorized as relating to either perceiving, processing, remembering, or responding to information. As examples, one cognitive style from each of these four categories is discussed.

Perceiving

A cognitive style concerned with perceiving is field independence versus field dependence. Field independence is characterized by analytical perception or responding to the important parts of a stimulus, while field dependence is characterized by global perception or responding to stimuli as a whole. Field independent students have a tendency to be reflective in responding and are less subject to the influences of social stimuli. This cognitive style has been found to be related to the cognitive abilities of general intelligence, verbal skills, and mathematical skills. The higher performance in these three areas is characteristic of students who are field independent. This cognitive style has also been found to be related to sex and to age, with females tending to be on the field dependent end of the continuum and older subjects tending to be on the field independent end of the continuum. There is also some indication that individuals who are on the field dependent end of the continuum are more sensitive and adaptive to social stimuli than those whose cognitive style is more field independent.

Processing

A cognitive style illustrative of a processing style is breadth of categorizing. Breadth of categorization refers to a preference for including many examples in a conceptual classification in contrast to a preference for limiting or confining the number of examples in a conceptual classification. It is thought that individuals who broadly categorize are more creative in problem solving because they include a wide variety of items or examples in a category and consequently are able to generate more possible solutions than the individual who narrowly categorizes. Either extreme in categorizing creates some risk to the individual student, the risk of errors in either inclusion or exclusion. It has been observed that individuals who prefer a broad categorization method have a tendency to shift to narrower categorization when the reward for correct classification becomes more desirable. At the present time in educational practice neither extreme of inclusiveness seems particularly valued, though correctness of categorization seems to be valued by the typical teacher.

Remembering

A cognitive style concerned with how individuals remember is leveling versus sharpening. This style refers to the manner in which individuals retain past experiences. Sharpeners tend to remember more details of past experience and maintain the separate identity and integrity of each experience in their memory. Levelers tend to remember vague impressions of past experiences and blend similar experiences in their memory. In learning activities involving memory, sharpeners make fewer errors than levelers because of their ability to remember details. Since many such activities occur in the classroom, sharpeners tend to do better in school. While movement toward the sharpening end of the continuum is observable in children as they grow older, the child's position on this continuum in relation to the child's peers remains relatively stable.

Children differ in the way they categorize.

Responding

Reflectivity versus impulsivity is a cognitive style concerned with the way individuals respond. Response speed and response errors are the characteristic factors involved in this style. Impulsive individuals respond quickly to an experience and make many errors. Reflective students think longer about an experience before responding and make few errors. Presently, both extremes on the continuum are considered detrimental to learning. Excessive impulsivity results

Some students prefer to learn through hearing, others through seeing, and still others through touching.

in responses without forethought. Excessive reflectivity results in a lack of responses. The middle range of the continuum in which response speed and response errors are balanced is considered most desirable. Research indicates that experience can produce changes on this continuum with some students. This instability is most evident at the extremes of the continuum. Experiences which produce change may be useful in the classroom for students at the extremes.

Another aspect of individual variation in the cognitive domain is termed sensory modality. Sensory modality refers to the preference individuals have for learning through a particular sense. Riessman (1964) suggests that there are three primary sensory modalities: kinesthetic, auditory, and visual. Some individuals may prefer and utilize whenever possible the "touch-feel-do" patterns of cognitive learning so often described as typical of the behavior of very young children. Others may rely heavily on auditory stimuli. Still others may emphasize the use of the visual modality. On the basis of nomothetic research, the ability to use the visual and auditory modes of learning appears to develop later than the ability to use a kinesthetic mode of learning. However, idiographic research suggests that once this development occurs, each individual prefers and utilizes one primary modality or a combination of modalities in a different way from other individuals.

In summary, the cognitive domain consists of the processes and/or products of human knowing. Individual differences in cognitive behavior are evident wherever one is willing to observe them. Some differences are distinguished by the demographic characteristics of individuals and some by the cognitive styles that individuals use in perceiving, processing, remembering, and responding to information. They are also present in the sensory modalities which individuals prefer and use as they learn to know themselves and their environment. Educational practices which are responsive to these differences are imperative for nurturing the abilities of individual children to their maximum potential.

Affective Domain

The affective domain consists of the feeling aspects of personal experiences. It includes the appreciations, attitudes, interests, and values of individuals which make them so interestingly different from or so pleasantly similar to other individuals. It also includes the emotional responses demonstrated by individuals as they contemplate themselves, their physical and ideational environment, and their interactions with other individuals or groups. Thus, development in the affective domain consists of movement toward maturity in both intrapsychic and social-psychological relationships.

Literature on affective development abounds with references concerning the interrelationship between these intrapsychic and social-psychological aspects. For example, Holt (1964), author of *How Children Fail*, states that highly anxious children often excessively fear embarrassment, disapproval, punishment, or the general lessening of their status. Combs and Snygg (1959) provide another example in their explanation of the effects of tension. They suggest that emotion is actually a tension state or a readiness to act, and that the degree of personal tension experienced will vary depending on the perceived relationship of the self to the situation, the clarity of the perception, the immediacy of the situation, and how adequately the individual feels able to cope with the situation. Thus, the intrapsychic and social-psychological aspects of affective development cannot be completely separated.

Affective development, like cognitive development, can be studied from a number of different dichotomized perspectives. These dichotomies of viewpoint include: (1) individual differences versus normative standards, (2) structure versus process, and (3) integration versus compartmentalization. They illustrate the difference between cognitive and affective development, as well as the distinct features which caused developmental theorists to separate these two domains of human behavior.

Individual Differences versus Normative Standards

One dichotomous perspective to the study of affective development emphasizes the similarities among individuals as opposed to the differences among individuals. Nomothetic research results in the identification of similarities among individuals as intrapsychic and social-psychological factors interact. An example of such a normative-based conclusion is that frustration, i.e., the behavioral outcome associated with the emotion of anger, leads to aggression. This normative-based conclusion would predict that a school-age child frustrated in learning mathematics would react aggressively. It does not, however, indicate much about the nature of the aggression. Idiographic research results in another type of data. Idiographic research would substantiate the existence of a relationship between frustration and aggression, but it would emphasize the unique differences among individuals' responses. The idiographic approach would predict that the child's uniqueness would dictate whether that child reacted: (1) symbolically or directly, (2) whether the child was able to control aggression by contemplating other factors involved in the situation, and (3) what the chosen target would be. Thus the research approaches complement each other. The normative approach is able to state a relationship. The idiographic approach is able to state how individuals perceive and process their own affective states and how these perceptions and processes are different from those of other individuals.

Structure versus Process

A second dichotomous perspective to the study of affective development takes a structural approach in contrast to a process approach. A structural approach emphasizes the sequential steps of affective development. An example from a structural-based theory is Freud's psychoanalytic-psychosexual stages. Affective development according to Freud proceeds through five stages: oral, anal, phallic, latent, and genital. A process approach, on the other hand, emphasizes the types of choices an individual makes in affective situations. An example from a process-based theory is a person's task-orientation or defense-orientation when that person is in a stress situation (Coleman 1972). Task-orientation occurs when the individual perceives a stress situation as nonthreatening to the self-concept the person possesses. The individual can decide whether the stress situation should be met, changed, or avoided without viewing any of these three choices as being devaluating. Defense-orientation occurs when an individual perceives a stress situation as a threat to the self. The individual's need to protect the self from devaluation influences the individual's ability to decide whether to meet, change, or avoid the situation, because one or more of these three choices may be degrading to the self-concept. Affective development according to a task-oriented theory occurs as an individual becomes more capable of focusing on the adjustment demands of a stress situation rather than by attempting to protect the self from devaluation in that situation. Like the individual differences versus normative standards perspective, the structural versus process perspective on affective development is complementary. The structural approach states when a particular affective development stage should be achieved. The process approach states how this achievement occurs.

Integration versus Compartmentalization

A third dichotomous approach to studying affective development arises when major focus is placed either upon integration of the self as an intrapsychic phenomenon or on compartmentalization of the personality as a social-psychological phenomenon. The sentence, "He's got his head together," means much to young people today. What is implied is that the person has resolved much of his intrapsychic dissonance. He knows what he is about. Integration of the personality is a goal of traditional psychoanalysis. Recently other theorists have begun to compartmentalize aspects of human affective behavior. One such group advocates what is called transactional analysis or TA. Here human affective behavior is divided into three parts: the child, the adult, and the parent that are present in all of us. The influence of these parts or roles seems to have much to do with the ways that an individual contemplates the self, the physical and ideational environment, and the individual's interaction with other individuals or groups.

Thus different theorists and practitioners choose different approaches in dealing with human affective development. These different approaches result because affective development is an extremely complex phenomenon. No matter what position is held, or which approach is advocated, affective development involves intrapsychic and social-psychological growth from (1) dependence to self-direction, (2) ignorance to self-knowledge, and (3) incompetence to competence. Each of these three is highly individual, and an educational system which attends to affective development must attend to that development in each individual child.

Psychomotor Domain

The psychomotor domain consists of those behaviors of individuals which have physical as well as mental components. Development in the psychomotor domain results from an interaction of physical, mental, and experiential factors which produce individuals who are similar in some ways and unique in others from their peers. Thus, an understanding of psychomotor development necessitates an understanding of physical growth and development as well as an understanding of the influence of mental and experiential factors on this development.

Psychomotor development, like cognitive and affective development, has been studied using both the nomothetic research method and the idiographic research method. The majority of research on physical growth and development has been done using the nomothetic method in attempting to find similarities in human development. Examples of similarities in physical development resulting from this type of research are the cephalocaudal and proximodistal developmental patterns. The cephalocaudal developmental pattern states that psychomotor control progresses from head to foot. Thus, an infant learns head control first, arm control next, and lastly, control of the legs and feet. The proximodistal development pattern states that psychomotor control progresses from the center of the body out to the extremities. Hence, a child learns to control the arms before learning to control the hands. The nomothetic approach to physical growth and development has applicability starting at birth, and is useful in discovering similarities in human development at all subsequent ages.

The research concerning the influence of experiential factors on physical growth and development has been done using both the nomothetic and idiographic method. Studies of large groups of children of the same chronological age, similar genetic endowment, and similar physical maturation, in relation to the development of specific motor skills, have shown that large differences occur among children and that motor skills are amenable to specific practice. Furthermore, this type of research has shown that amount of practice influences the extent of one's ability in any motor skill, and that amount of practice may be influenced by a wide variety of sources such as the individual's family status, the parents' expectations, cultural norms, early reinforcement, and sex-based rules for play.

Idiographic research concerning the influence of experiential factors has been applied to specific skill areas and resulted in conclusions complementary to the conclusions reached through nomothetic research. For example, the study of precocious musicians reveals that a parent with high expectations who demands and reinforces specific practice on the musical instrument is often a dominant figure in the musician's life. Thus, just as research in the cognitive and affective domains revealed a utility of information from both nomothetic and idiographic research, this is also true in the psychomotor domain.

Particular psychomotor skills are manifested by all individuals as they interact with their environment. Mobility and speech are two of the most obvious skills in which a human's similarity to and difference from other humans is observable. These similarities and differences may result from family, culture, sex, genetics, learning, or many other factors. Research in the psychomotor domain is directed at discovering these factors and the factors which foster competency in the psychomotor area. The teacher should be aware that individual differences do exist in this area, and plan children's educational experiences to maximize their particular psychomotor abilities and styles, especially in the areas of human interaction, such as speech and mobility.

Summary

In summary, individual differences are apparent in cognitive, affective, and psychomotor development. A prospective teacher who believes that all six-year-olds, or all children with IQ scores one standard deviation above the mean, or all children from lower sociometric families are quite similar would likely be shocked and perplexed upon actually

observing a normal classroom of individual children. Cutts and Mose-
ley (1960), describing an actual typical sixth grade class of twenty-
nine pupils, dramatically depict the wide range of individual differences a teacher may expect to find in a classroom. For example, the
students differed in chronological age more than three and one-half
years, in weight more than one hundred pounds, in height fourteen
inches, on IQ scores sixty points, and on standardized achievement
tests five and one-half grades. The class included students from all
socioeconomic strata. They differed in work and leisure experiences,
family socialization structure, parental expectations, self-conscious-
ness, cheerfulness, precision, temperament, and physical skills. Thus
individual differences in cognitive, affective, and psychomotor behavior are an important aspect of human development to be considered
in the educational process.

The vast range of individual differences present in students in
the three domains of human performance makes evident the fact that
these differences must be taken into account in educational planning.

The real strength of IGE is its ability to provide for the unique strengths and
weaknesses of each individual learner.

With what type of an educational system should individuals interact? What type of educational system is most likely to allow students to achieve their maximum potential? Instruction designed for the average or even the majority of students hasn't allowed the maximum to be reached by all students. Even instructional programs which group children homogeneously according to one ability do not provide for variation and difference in other abilities. How then can teachers teach and students learn efficiently? One answer supported by developmental research is that an efficient learning situation is tailored to the specific needs, abilities, learning styles, and expectations of the individual student. It is believed that only when an educational environment is designed specifically for an individual can that individual fully interact with it and thereby realize that individual's unique potential. IGE is such an environment.

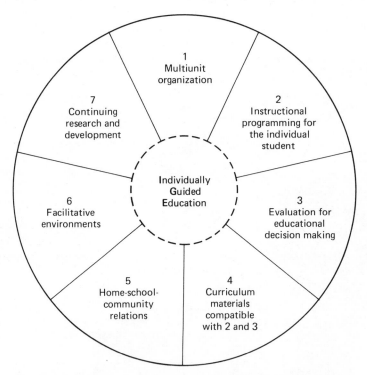

Fig. 2.1 Components of individually guided education. Based on H. J. Klausmeier, M. R. Quilling, J. S. Sorenson, R. S. Way, and G. R. Glasrud 1971. *Individually guided education and the multiunit elementary school: guidelines for implementation.* Madison, Wisc.: Wisconsin Research and Development Center for Cognitive Learning, Ch. 2.

PRIMARY COMPONENTS OF INDIVIDUALLY GUIDED EDUCATION

IGE (Klausmeier 1975) consists of a total learning environment which is designed to meet the uniqueness of the individual students. Figure 2.1 indicates the seven major components of IGE. These consist of (1) multiunit organization, (2) instructional programming for the individual student, (3) evaluation for educational decision making, (4) curriculum materials compatible with 2 and 3, (5) home-school-community relations, (6) facilitative environments, and (7) continuing research and development. Each IGE school has all the components.

Multiunit Organizational-administrative Arrangements

The multiunit organizational-administrative arrangements are concepts in organizational structure and educational practice that have evolved from successful past educational practice and contemporary theory related to organizational structure, management, communication, and decision making. The purpose of the organizational administrative arrangements is to enhance the learning of each individual student.

Organizational Structure and Management

The organizational structure is designed to promote efficient management and effective communication in multiunit schools. It can be applied to particular schools with few minor alterations. The alterations needed in terms of number and type of school personnel available as well as number of students in attendance are provided for in the organizational plan. Figure 2.2 depicts a prototypic organizational chart for a typical multiunit school of 600 students. From this illustration it may be inferred how organizational modifications for particular schools can be made so as to implement components (2) through (7) of the model depicted in Figure 2.1.

The organizational structure is hierarchical. At the highest level is the systemwide program committee consisting of the district administrator, central office consultants, a community representative, and representative teachers, unit leaders, and principals of IGE and other schools. The systemwide program committee functions initially to facilitate the transition of conventional schools to IGE schooling and is responsible for (1) recruitment of personnel for each IGE school, (2) inservice education activities, (3) provision of instructional materials and other logistic functions, and (4) dissemination of relevant information within the school district and community. Once there are several IGE schools, the systemwide program com-

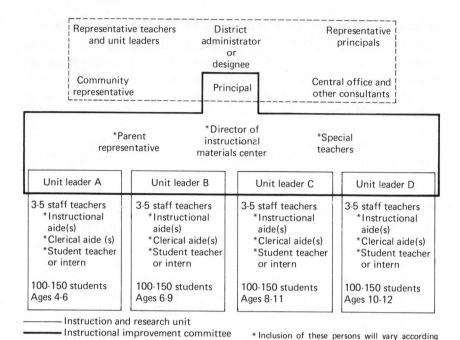

Representative teachers and unit leaders	District administrator or designee	Representative principals
Community representative	Principal	Central office and other consultants

*Parent representative	*Director of instructional materials center	*Special teachers

Unit leader A	Unit leader B	Unit leader C	Unit leader D
3-5 staff teachers *Instructional aide(s) *Clerical aide (s) *Student teacher or intern 100-150 students Ages 4-6	3-5 staff teachers *Instructional aide(s) *Clerical aide(s) *Student teacher or intern 100-150 students Ages 6-9	3-5 staff teachers *Instructional aide(s) *Clerical aide(s) *Student teacher or intern 100-150 students Ages 8-11	3-5 staff teachers *Instructional aide(s) *Clerical aide(s) *Student teacher or intern 100-150 students Ages 10-12

———— Instruction and research unit
▬▬▬ Instructional improvement committee
------- Systemwide program committee

* Inclusion of these persons will vary according to particular school settings.

Fig. 2.2 Multiunit organization of an IGE school of 400–600 students. Adapted from H. J. Klausmeier, R. G. Morrow, and J. E. Walter 1968. *Individually guided education in the multiunit elementary school: guidelines for implementation.* Madison, Wisc.: Wisconsin Research and Development Center for Cognitive Learning.

mittee may continue to function for these reasons and also as an informational-exchange agency and for general policy and supervisory functions.

The second level in the organizational hierarchy is the Instructional Improvement Committee (IIC) which consists of the building principal and the unit leaders. It often includes a parent representative, special teachers, and the director of the instructional materials center, and also often is the focus for input from external consultants. The IIC functions primarily to interpret and implement systemwide policies, to coordinate unit activities, and to provide for independent use of facilities, time, and materials by instructional units.

The Instruction and Research Unit (I & R Unit) reflects the dual and related tasks of the teachers, i.e., providing instruction, and doing the research and evaluation which is necessary to ensure a quality individualized instructional program for each child. This nongraded I & R Unit actually replaces the traditional age-graded self-contained classroom. Each unit is designed to have a unit leader, staff teachers, and sometimes instructional aides, clerical aides, and a teacher-intern. It may have between 75 and 200 students. The exact number and type of instructional personnel in each unit varies based upon the needs and the number of students in each unit.

This differentiated staffing within each unit facilitates the development, implementation, and evaluation of instructional programs for individual students. The unit leader, an individual selected because of outstanding leadership qualities as well as instructional excellence, coordinates personnel, materials, and resources. The unit leader serves as a liaison between the unit staff and other school personnel, in addition to directly teaching children. The staff teachers plan, implement, and evaluate the instruction. Their job responsibilities demand more professional and less routine work than is demanded of the teacher in traditional schools. Staff teachers take the initiative and responsibility for instruction in the content or methodology areas of their strengths. However, in a multiunit structure, staff teachers do not act as specialists, but rather they gain in experience and understanding of their initially weaker curricular areas through interstaff communication and inservice education programs. In addition to the unit teacher and the staff teacher, other staff personnel are available in IGE schools to facilitate the instructional activities that go on in each unit.

Communication and Decision Making

The IGE schools are characterized by open communication and shared decision making. As in other successful organizations, accountability is of importance. In the IGE school accountability for action moves in a rising vertical linear direction, that is, the staff teacher is accountable to the lead teacher who is accountable to the unit principal, etc. On the other hand, decision making in the multiunit school is not limited to the top to bottom linear direction. Although some decision making does occur in that direction, much occurs in the opposite direction. For example, the staff for each unit identifies needs of children in that unit and the total staff decides how their efforts can be directed toward meeting these needs. Thus the knowledge and expertise of all personnel is utilized in IGE schools.

Because of these differences between IGE schools and traditional schools, school personnel in IGE schools see their job responsibilities as different from those of personnel from traditional schools (Klausmeier and Pellegrin 1971). IGE school personnel more often recognize their role in planning and preparation whereas traditional school personnel more often recognize their role in terms of discipline, supervision, and correction of student work. Also the IGE teachers tend to specialize more than the traditional teachers. This specialization occurs in a wide variety of areas including content, instructional methodology, and grouping practices. Teachers in IGE schools are more involved in team efforts than their colleagues in traditional schools who appear to be relatively isolated. Thus, the communication and decision-making structure of the IGE school appears to be more effective than that found in more traditional schools.

Although such findings may speak directly to professional enhancement and morale of teachers, they are useless unless data also reveal that teachers do indeed pay close attention to students as individuals. Again, Klausmeier and Pellegrin (1971) found that IGE teachers and traditional teachers, when asked to choose three out of eleven listed operational goals as being most vital to their work, chose different goals. In contrast to the development of basic skills and analytic reasoning which were important goals to the traditional school teachers, the IGE teachers selected individual attention to students and diagnosing learning problems of students as being the most important goals of teachers. Thus it is apparent that the organization and operation of IGE schools can effectively provide a structure within which teachers are free to plan, implement, and evaluate individualized instruction and to be professionally and personally rewarded for doing so. In such a setting, each student who marches to the beat of a different drummer will be encouraged and assisted to develop and to learn in step with the tempo which that student hears.

Other Primary Components of IGE

As a learning environment designed to meet the unique needs of individual students, the IGE school is more than an organizational structure. As a total system, IGE has additional components which make it possible to facilitate the development of individual students.

The second component is the model of instructional programming for the individual student. It is through the application of this model that provision is made for individual differences such as those related to rate of learning, interests, motivation levels, style of learning, and prior achievement. It is this component which is the heart of individually guided educational programming practices in IGE schools.

The instructional programming model which coordinates all the educational efforts is depicted in Figure 2.3. This figure suggests that all of the components are inherently related. Implementation of the instructional programming model initially requires the setting of

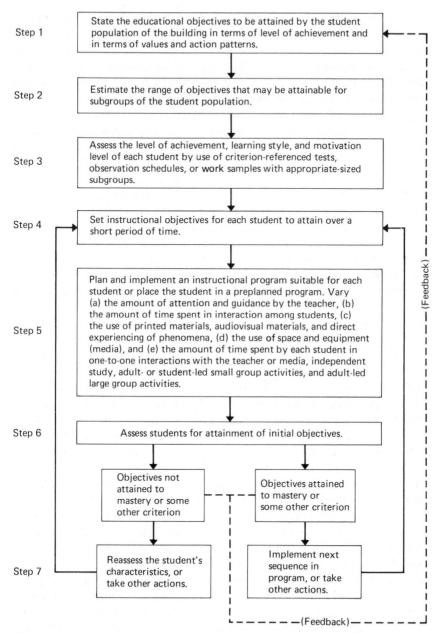

Step 1 — State the educational objectives to be attained by the student population of the building in terms of level of achievement and in terms of values and action patterns.

Step 2 — Estimate the range of objectives that may be attainable for subgroups of the student population.

Step 3 — Assess the level of achievement, learning style, and motivation level of each student by use of criterion-referenced tests, observation schedules, or work samples with appropriate-sized subgroups.

Step 4 — Set instructional objectives for each student to attain over a short period of time.

Step 5 — Plan and implement an instructional program suitable for each student or place the student in a preplanned program. Vary (a) the amount of attention and guidance by the teacher, (b) the amount of time spent in interaction among students, (c) the use of printed materials, audiovisual materials, and direct experiencing of phenomena, (d) the use of space and equipment (media), and (e) the amount of time spent by each student in one-to-one interactions with the teacher or media, independent study, adult- or student-led small group activities, and adult-led large group activities.

Step 6 — Assess students for attainment of initial objectives.

Objectives not attained to mastery or some other criterion

Objectives attained to mastery or some other criterion

Step 7 — Reassess the student's characteristics, or take other actions.

Implement next sequence in program, or take other actions.

(Feedback)

(Feedback)

Fig. 2.3 Instructional programming model in IGE. Adapted from H. J. Klausmeier, M. R. Quilling, J. S. Sorenson, R. S. Way, and G. R. Glasrud 1971. *Individually guided education and the multiunit elementary school: guidelines for implementation.* Madison, Wisc.: Wisconsin Research and Development Center for Cognitive Learning, p. 19.

reasonable long-range objectives to be attained by all students so that the development of a subrange of objectives for specified groups of students can be undertaken (Steps 1 and 2). The programming model next requires specific short-term objectives to be set for each individual learner based upon the assessment of the individual's own entry level, motivational level, and learning style (Steps 3 and 4). These individual short-term objectives are made with consideration given to the consensually validated set of long-range objectives for the student population as a whole.

After the objective stage in the implementation of the programming model is met, the planning and execution of an instructional program which is appropriate for each individual begins. It is here that research and development activities bear major importance. The model is designed to implement the most effective ways of teaching facts, concepts, and skills specified in the individual learner's set of short-term instructional objectives. In practice, individual variation would be evident in the amount of direct guidance offered by the teacher, the amount and type of interaction with other students, the number and kind of different curriculum materials used, and the amount of independent study in which a given student might be involved (Step 5).

After the planning and implementation of a particular child's instructional program is completed, the summative assessment stage begins (Steps 6 and 7). At this stage the teaching team determines what each child has learned, primarily by the use of criterion-referenced tests based on short-term objectives, as well as by the use of other validated assessment techniques. At this point, the model provides for a decision based upon the results of the assessment. In a mastery-based sequenced program, if the objectives have been met by the learner, new individual short-term objectives for each child are then agreed upon by the learner, the teacher, or the staff, and the cycle starts again. On the other hand, if the original mastery objectives have not been met by the learner, a reassessment of the student's characteristics is then made, again investigating the learner's individual style, entry level, and motivational characteristics. Then the original short-term objectives are modified to be more appropriate for the abilities and interests of the individual learner. Emphasis is placed upon revising the instructional program for that individual learner so that the learner's objectives may now be met by other and more appropriate means.

It should be apparent that many objectives in the affective and psychomotor domains do not call for a particular level of mastery by all students. Rather, each child attains a level which the teachers judge appropriate for the particular child. Instructional programming for the individual student deals with these objectives also as noted in Figure 2.3.

CONSONANCE OF INDIVIDUALLY GUIDED EDUCATION WITH DEVELOPMENTAL THEORY

Viewed in its entirety, IGE seems consonant with the developmental perspective which views the individual as an interactive agent. Through the process of short-term goal setting and the educational practices which implement achievement of these goals, the learner-teacher interaction is not only individualized, it becomes personalized. Learner-teacher and learner-learner communications both are enhanced by the very design of the program. Both learners and teachers are allowed freedom in decisions about the regulation of themselves and the learning environment.

The programming model also attends to both innate and experiential factors in the development of each individual learner. It recognizes that development implies progress toward maturity and that to a degree such maturity is specified a priori in terms of genetic endowment. On the other hand it recognizes that environmental factors influence development, and it provides supportive experience in terms of the individual's capabilities, needs, motivation, and interests. Thus the model provides for both hereditary and environmental considerations.

Providing for Commonalities in Children's Development

Commonalities in the development of children have long been recognized. Historically, traditional education has tended to overestimate and overemphasize these commonalities. For example, age-grade placement of children was practiced because of similarities in children of the same age. This was modified because all children of the same chronological age didn't demonstrate the same abilities. Homogeneous grouping was next tried, with similar results. Children grouped for all their instruction on the basis of one criterion such as mental age were found to reflect almost as great a variation in another variable such as social development as when homogeneous grouping was not used. Thus although the effort of traditional education to group children has become desirable for administrative purposes, its ability to provide for their commonalities has essentially been a failure.

IGE provides for different commonalities in children's learning than those commonalities traditional schools have focused upon to date. Traditional schools have focused upon arbitrary and artificial criteria such as age, IQ score, or overall achievement level. IGE focuses upon commonalities such as style of learning, motivation, interest, and readiness for specific material to be learned. Thus, IGE does not imply that all learning is attained in isolation. Commonalities in the development of children are recognized. The educational personnel in the IGE school realize that it may be preferable for a given student to learn some material by reading alone, other material by involvement in group activities, and yet other material through interaction with a simulator or one other person. Depending upon the needs and preferences of the children being considered, homogeneous grouping either in large or small groups may be the best means of implementation in one instance, while heterogeneous grouping may be more effective in another situation. The most effective methods for particular children at particular times in their development can only be determined by continuous reassessment of the learner and the learning situation, a process which is continually practiced in Individually Guided Education.

Providing for Differences in Children's Development

The real strength of Individually Guided Education is its ability to provide for the unique strengths and weaknesses of each individual learner whether they are the result of innate, experiential, or interactive factors. Provision is made in IGE schools for each individual to learn in that individual's own preferred modality. Differences in the styles of children's learning are taken into account when selecting short-term objectives and when determining how these objectives are to be attained. The developmental stage at which the learner is functioning is also considered in these activities as are other intellectual factors. The motivational level of the learner is evaluated as objectives are selected. Also at this time, the specific interests of that individual are considered. The instructional objectives and instructional program are then specifically selected and designed for that individual. Thus the unique perceptions of all individuals are taken into account as their learning experiences are cooperatively planned by both the teachers and themselves.

In summary, IGE with instructional programming for the individual student is a departure from the traditional age-graded school. It has unique organizational arrangements and educational practices which provide educational experiences for children which are consonant with developmental theory. It not only provides for the commonalities in the ways that pupils learn and develop, but more importantly, it provides for the unique differences in the ways children learn and develop.

INSTRUCTIONAL PROGRAMMING IN INDIVIDUALLY GUIDED EDUCATION SCHOOLS

The teachers in IGE schools critically examine and provide for individual differences in learners' cognitive, affective, and psychomotor behaviors. The third step of the programming model (Fig. 2.3) specifically requires an assessment of the "level of achievement, learning styles, and motivational level of each student by use of criterion-referenced tests, observation schedules, and work samples . . ." That is, prior to setting specific short-term instructional objectives, an assessment is made of each student's initial achievement level in terms of the cognitive, affective, and psychomotor behavior the student is capable of performing. Also, the student's learning style and motivational level for new learning in each domain are assessed.

Level of achievement refers to learning outcomes in the three domains. In the cognitive domain, the learning outcomes are facts, concepts, and cognitive skills. In the affective domain, learning outcomes are appreciations, attitudes, interests, and values. In the psychomotor domain, the outcomes are motor performances such as body manipulations, vocal skills, hand-eye coordination, etc. Assessment of a level of achievement refers to an appraisal of what learning outcomes students already have in their behavioral repertoire and those behaviors that next would be logical for them to acquire.

Assessment of motivational level consists of more than simply determining if a child would be interested in working on certain specific short-term objectives. Rather, it involves estimating the extent to which the child attends to and persists in learning activities designed to attain the objectives. Further, the motivation deals not only with cognitive activities but also with conduct and social relationships.

Assessment of learning style involves a variety of alternatives related to the efficiency with which individual students learn through different instructional arrangements and processes. Students who demonstrate independence, the ability to read and comprehend what they read, the ability to use audiovisual materials, and the ability to evaluate their own performance, are very different from students who demonstrate dependence, limited knowledge and skills, and little self-evaluative ability. Instructional arrangements for the first type of student, of necessity, must be markedly different from the second, if each student is to be helped to become that which each is capable of being.

It is on the basis of the assessments of achievement level, motivational level, and learning style that an instructional program for each individual can be planned and implemented. Each program is attentive to the outcomes of individual assessments through the utilization of variation in the instructional factors of the fifth component in the instructional programming model. These factors, as presented in Figure 2.3, are (1) the amount of attention and guidance by the teacher, (2) the amount of time spent in interaction among students, (3) the use of printed materials, audiovisual materials, and direct experience, (4) the use of space and equipment (media), and (5) the amount of time spent by each student in one-to-one interactions with the teacher or media, independent study, adult- or student-led small group activities, and adult-led large group activities. These and other factors are taken into account as instructional programs are implemented to foster student development in the cognitive, affective, and psychomotor domains.

Cognitive Domain

In the cognitive domain, the specific differences in cognitive style should be considered during instructional planning and implementation. Individual learners may be assessed with regard to the nine dimensions of cognitive styles as described by Messick (1969). Some of this assessment can be accomplished by utilization of available testing instruments specifically designed to measure one or more dimensions of cognitive style. Other assessments can be made by careful observation of the child during the act of learning. Still other assessments can be made through records of the child's developmental history and experiential background. Thus, an educator can determine, for example, whether the student learns better through a global or an analytic approach and whether this is characteristic of the student's general learning style or the learning style in specific content or performance areas.

Do students attend to many stimuli in their environment or do they generally attend only to narrow dimensions of their environment? Similarly, do the students include a wide variety of examples in a category or do they tend to maintain a narrow breadth of categorization? Do these two factors have an effect on their willingness to creatively attack problems? Should other factors be considered in planning problem-solving activities for students? When confronted with a new learning situation, does the individual student tend to be impulsive or reflective in approaching the situation? When recalling or applying what the student learned, does the student clearly retain the details of past learning or do the details become vague and distorted by other learning experiences in the student's memory? Is the student comfortable in new learning situations which appear to be incongruent with past situations, or do past situations hamper the student's ability to learn in the new situation?

Assessment of specific cognitive styles may appear to be an overwhelming task to the new teacher who operates within the confines of the traditional classroom setting. However, with the unit approach in IGE schools, and with adequate planning, the assessment of individual cognitive styles can be accomplished.

Such assessment is essential to the development of appropriate instructional strategies for individual children. Thus, individualized assessment is an integral part of the implementation of instructional programming within the multiunit school. Without such assessment, the program is inoperative.

What, then, does the educator do after assessment has been made? Again, the answer is to plan and carry out an instructional program appropriate for the individual student. For example, it may be that the students could be grouped according to their preferred cognitive style in specific content areas and/or matched with teachers who also prefer that style or whose instructional styles complement the learner's style. Such matching of teacher with student has been suggested (Rubin 1973). On the other hand, individual learning may be enhanced by assisting the learner to modify a preferred style or at least to alter it sufficiently to better understand and learn concepts, or develop skills in specific areas. In this regard, IGE operates within a prescriptive format.

As in assessing and utilizing each student's cognitive style for specific instructional programming, an educative team can also assess the preferred sensory modality of each student through systematic observation, and arrange to utilize it in instructional programming. That is, objectives can be set for specific concept learning that utilize sensory-kinesthetic (role-playing, model-building) materials, visual (films, books, demonstrations) materials, and/or auditory (tape recordings, lectures) materials. Of course, each student would not be expected to learn only via the student's preferred sensory modality. This would not allow the student to develop potential learning abilities. On the other hand, the student would not be expected to utilize in isolation a modality which is not appropriate for the student. This would not allow the student to develop potential in terms of cognitive behavior.

Affective Domain

The affective domain of individuals can also be readily assessed by educative teams. With the development of an effective working relationship with the learner, and with careful observation of that learner in a variety of settings, the team can determine those situations in which the learner appears to be more or less anxious, motivated, affectionate, fearful, defensive, confident, etc. An understanding of how the student's affective development influences cognitive and psychomotor performances will aid the educative team in determining the appropriate learning settings for each student. For example, a student who is quite ill at ease in a large group setting may learn at a faster rate and with greater interest if the learning takes place in a small group, a one-to-one, or an individual setting. Affective development can also be encouraged through proper manipulation of learning environments. For example, the student who is ill at ease in a large group setting may initially be placed in a small group setting, but at later times moved to increasingly larger groups. Thus, the learning settings and instructional materials can be adjusted for individual students to provide situations in which each learner can develop the learner's full cognitive and affective potential.

Psychomotor Domain

Because of the known effect of practice on the development of specific psychomotor skills, assessment in the psychomotor domain must focus on both intraindividual differences and interindividual differences. Intraindividual differences are differences in psychomotor skills within a particular individual. For example, a particular student may have difficulty learning to write during the same period in which the same student is able to do artwork or model building with ease. Interindividual differences are differences in psychomotor skills among individuals. For example, one student may have difficulty learning to write, while another student learns to write quickly and with ease. Both intraindividual differences and interindividual differences can occur in any area of psychomotor development. Their existence in areas of locomotion, writing, drawing, and other educational activities which call for gross and/or fine motor capabilities should be recognized and assessed. Assessment in the psychomotor domain is predominantly performed through acute observation with the aid of checklists, suggested activities to observe, etc. Assessment in the psychomotor domain allows the intraindividual and interindividual differences of students to be provided for through selection of instructional materials and settings suitable to each student.

In summary, IGE is designed to provide for individual differences in the cognitive, affective, and psychomotor domains. Assessment of differences in all three domains is required by the instructional programming model. The knowledge gained through assessment is used in setting specific short-term instructional objectives and planning and implementing a program designed to foster development in the cognitive, affective, and psychomotor domains. Thus, the uniqueness of the individual student is provided for in IGE.

INDIVIDUALLY GUIDED EDUCATION AS A REFLECTION OF SOCIETAL VALUES

Should education in America be based on simplicity, the inertia of the status quo, and the maintenance of minimal economic investment? Or should the democratic principle of equality of opportunity be accepted, and an educational opportunity provided for all individuals to develop their maximum potential? Democratic education cannot be simplistic. Change must replace the status quo, and economic and human resources must be directed toward improvement of the quality of educational opportunity for each individual child. IGE is not simplistic. It utilizes all the knowledge obtained from the complexity of present-day society. It requires a change from the status quo of traditional education. It requires that economic and human resources be directed toward improvement of the quality of education offered each child.

The multiunit organizational arrangement with instructional programming for the individual student is being implemented in hundreds of school systems across the country. The program's rapid adoption by boards of education, school personnel, and communities is a reflection of the democratic values it engenders. It provides for individual differences. Each individual is allowed to learn at a rate which is appropriate for that individual and allowed to progress to a level of achievement which is consonant with personal ability. The program fosters responsibility in each individual student, preparing that student for participation in a democracy. The value of learning as a lifelong process is better understood by a child who is fortunate enough to experience a program of IGE tailored to meet individual needs and abilities.

People learn not only what they are formally taught but also through imitation, examples, and models. An excited, responsible, involved, cooperative, inquisitive, and motivated school staff will informally teach these characteristics to their students. Since team members of IGE schools are given greater responsibility for their own actions and accomplishments, communication and teamwork is manifested by the team members. The resulting changes in teacher attitudes and increased instructional efforts by teachers are good experiences for children. They result in imitation learning of attitude which better prepare students to achieve happy and successful lives.

In IGE, major attention is given to the development of a systematic program of parent-child-school interaction. A parent is included in the Instructional Improvement Committee (IIC). Home visits may be made by teachers and unit leaders, thus enabling two-way communications designed to increase the understanding of the child, the system, and their interaction. Community leaders and central staff personnel elected or appointed are included in the development, interpretation, and implementation of systemwide policies designed to achieve individualized education. Thus, rather than further alienating the school from the community and the teacher from the family, IGE actually enhances their interaction. Such involvement and interaction closely matches the democratic American society in which each student will one day be involved.

Thus the implementation of IGE operates within the value framework of our democratic society, the essence of which is respect for the individual person. The IGE school operates as a humanizing agent. It is when each learner understands that each is accepted as an independent and important individual that each, in turn, is able to also accept others as such. The IGE programming model within the multiunit school, by its very design, is based upon the concept that while individuals may differ, all individuals are important and worthwhile.

SUGGESTED READINGS FOR CHAPTER 2

Wallace, J. G. 1965. *Concept growth and the education of the child.* London: The National Foundation for Educational Research in England and Wales.

This book broadly interprets the traditional concepts of growth and development as espoused by theorists such as Skinner, Harlow, and Bruner. Special attention is given to the work of Piaget and to ways of applying developmental theories in instructional programming for the individual student.

Holt, J. C. 1964. *How children fail.* New York: Pitman.

Holt tries to give insight into the ways children try to meet or dodge school demands of adults. He explores the interaction in children of fear and failure, as well as the differences in what children appear to know, what they are expected to know, and what they really know. An analysis of the ways in which schools increase children's fears, produce fragmented, distorted, and short-lived learning, and fail to meet the real needs of children, is also contained in this book.

Klausmeier, H. J. 1971. An alternative form of schooling. In D. S. Bushnell and D. Rappaport (eds.), *Planned change in education.* New York: Harcourt.

Klausmeier believes that IGE has proven to be one effective alternative to the age-graded, self-contained classroom in the elementary and middle school. He extensively describes the seven major components of IGE's organization and operation, which were specifically designed to produce higher educational achievement by providing for differences among students in rate of learning, learning style, and other characteristics.

REFERENCES

Allport, G. W. 1961. *Pattern and growth in personality.* New York: Holt.

Beard, R. M. 1961. *A study of number concepts in the infants school.* Prepublication draft of report on behalf of A.T.C.D.E. Mathematics Section.

Bushnell, D. S. and D. Rappaport (eds.) 1971. *Planned change in education.* New York: Harcourt.

Coleman, J. C. 1972. *Abnormal psychology and modern life.* (4th ed.) Glenview, Ill.: Scott Foresman.

Combs, A. W., and D. Snygg 1959. *Individual behavior: a perceptual approach to behavior.* (rev. ed.) New York: Harper & Row.

Cutts, N. E., and N. Mosely 1960. *Providing for individual differences in the elementary school.* Englewood Cliffs, N.J.: Prentice-Hall.

Holt, J. C. 1964. *How children fail.* New York: Pitman.

Holzman, S. 1972. *IGE: individually guided education and the multiunit school.* (Education USA Special Report) Arlington, Va.: National School Public Relations Association.

Hood, H. B. 1962. An experimental study of Piaget's theory of the development of number in children. *British Journal of Psychology* 53: 273–286.

Klausmeier, H. J. 1975. *IGE: An alternative form of schooling.* In H. Talmage (ed.), *Systems of individualized education.* Berkeley, Calif.: McCutchan.

———, and R. J. Pellegrin 1971. The multiunit school: A differential staffing approach. In D. S. Bushnell and D. Rappaport (eds.), *Planned change in education.* New York: Harcourt.

———, 1971. The multiunit elementary school and individually guided education. *Phi Beta Kappan* 53: 181–184.

———, M. R. Quilling, J. S. Sorenson, R. S. Way, and G. R. Glasrud 1971. *Individually guided education and the multiunit elementary school: guidelines for implementation.* Madison, Wisc.: Wisconsin Research and Development Center for Cognitive Learning.

———, R. Morrow, and J. E. Walter 1968. *Individually guided education in the multiunit elementary school: guidelines for implementation.* Madison: Wisconsin Department of Public Instruction.

Messick, S. 1969. *The criterion problem in the education of instruction.* Princeton, N.J.: Educational Testing Services.

Piaget, J. 1963. *The origins of intelligence in children.* New York: Norton.

Rappaport, D. 1972. *Personality development.* Glenview, Ill.: Scott Foresman.

Reissman, F. 1964. The strategy of style. *Teachers College Record* 65: 484–489.

Rubin, L. J. 1973. Matching teacher, student, and method. *Todays Education* 62 (6): 31–35.

Wallace, J. G. 1965. *Concept growth and the education of the child.* London: The National Foundation for Educational Research in England and Wales.

Wittrock, M. D. and D. E. Wiley (eds.) 1970. *The evaluation of instruction: issues and problems.* New York: Holt.

3

Cognitive Development

Objectives

Upon completion of this chapter, the reader should be able:

- To define and give examples of cognitive development.
- To distinguish and articulate the differences between cognitive-stage theory and cumulative-learning theory.
- To demonstrate an understanding of Piaget's theory, articulating his stages of development and the behavior which is indicative that an individual is at a particular stage of development.
- To demonstrate an understanding of Bruner's theory, articulating his stages of development and the behavior which is indicative that an individual is at a particular stage of development.
- To analyze the ways that cumulative-learning theorists differ from stage theorists in terms of the contributions of Gagne, Skinner, Bruner, and Piaget.
- To analyze the ways that cognitive development may be facilitated through the multiunit school and its individually guided educational programming model.

> *If we are satisfied with our present system, the application of knowledge about learning can only refine the preparation of textbooks and the nature of teacher procedures; it cannot be expected to demonstrate improvement of great magnitude. In contrast, the full exploitation of learning knowledge is possible in a newly designed system of education which focuses attention upon the individual learner and his continued development.*
>
> Gagne*

THEORIES OF DEVELOPMENT

Teachers have one of the most difficult jobs in the world. An architect can make a blueprint and a mechanic can replace a part on a car, but a teacher can't 'learn' anyone. All a teacher can do is help students to learn. How to provide this help in the most suitable manner requires that a teacher knows about the raw material with which the teacher works. It also requires that given raw material of a particular kind, the teacher is able to create with it something that was not there before. As such, a teacher is both a scientist and an artist; a scientist because of knowledge of the true nature of the raw material and ways of working with it, an artist because the teacher creates in each individual a desire to learn and become that which the individual is capable of being. A teacher produces in students a desire to learn those facts, concepts, and skills which have been shown to be necessary for humans to interact satisfactorily with their environment. A teacher creates competent individuals who go on learning after leaving the classroom.

In order to develop competence in students, teachers must be competent themselves and must understand the nature of human development, the nature of the raw material with which they work. The purpose of this chapter on cognitive development is to provide teachers with knowledge and understanding of the cognitive nature of students, knowledge which will aid teachers in developing the cognitive potentials of their students and enable them to become the creator of their own destinies.

Cognition is both the process and the product of knowing, and cognitive development is the growth demonstrated by human beings as they progress from a state of not knowing to knowing. What is the nature of human cognitive development? What type of educational

---

* R. M. Gagne 1966. Elementary science: "a new scheme of instruction." *Science* 151 (January): 49–53.

experiences will provide for optimal cognitive development? These questions have been contemplated by educators and psychologists and have resulted in two different theoretical positions which explain cognitive development. These positions are termed cognitive stage theories and cumulative learning theories.

Cognitive stage theories developed as a reaction against behaviorism. Cognitivists believed that the behaviorists' explanation of human behavior in terms of stimulus-response bonds was too simplistic and not applicable to higher mental processes. Consequently, cognitive psychologists developed theories to help explain higher mental processes such as knowing, information processing, decision making, and problem solving. Principles of cognitive behavior have been used by these psychologists to formulate theories of human development. Thus development, according to the cognitivists, is the change that occurs in an individual's cognitive or intellectual structure as that individual interacts with the environment. Such theories usually view development as a discontinuous process. The individual is regarded as a somewhat different organism at each stage of the individual's development.

Cumulative learning theories consider human development to be a continuous, ongoing process. Such theorists maintain that prior learning is the major determinant of cognitive development as contrasted to the innately regulated stages emphasized by the stage theorists. What one learns, according to this approach, is added on to what one already knows in a building-block manner. Innate organismic changes are not acknowledged as important in human development.

Various stage and cumulative learning theories have been proposed to explain cognitive development. This chapter presents and discusses some of the more familiar of each, and explores some of the implications that these theories of development have for educational experiences in the multiunit school.

STAGE THEORIES OF DEVELOPMENT

Theoretical Approach of Jean Piaget

Jean Piaget (1963), a Swiss psychologist known for his studies in child development, is a cognitive theorist. Piaget uses a child's different abilities to reason or use logic at different periods of the child's life to divide the course of human development into four structural stages. Cognitive development is a continuous interactive process, but because of the innate changes in individuals' cognitive operations and structures at these different stages, there is evidence of discontinuity among Piaget's stages.

Assumptions of Piaget's Theory

Because Piaget recognizes that both heredity and experience play important roles in human development his theory reflects an interactionist viewpoint. For instance, abilities such as walking or talking, acquired at various stages in development, require certain genetic factors. However, the age at which a child will reach a particular stage is a function of both innate and experiential factors. It is possible, according to Piaget's theory, that an infant possesses all of the necessary genetic traits and innate factors for coordination, and yet is not able to manipulate objects because it has been deprived of playthings necessary for the development of such skills.

Besides assuming the interaction of heredity and environment, Piaget assumes that people have a natural tendency to know and will actively work to extend their knowledge. It is for this reason that people interact with their environment. Piaget believes that the learning experience of interacting with one's environment must be fit into an already existing intellectual framework or some type of change in cognitive structure must result. This is what Piaget refers to as cognitive development.

Another assumption made in Piaget's theory is that all living organisms share two things in common: organization and adaptation. These two biological characteristics make up the core of human functioning. Piaget claims that every organism tends to integrate experiences into coherent systems. This is what Piaget refers to as organization. The second characteristic, adaptation, is the innate tendency of an organism to interact with its environment.

According to Piaget's stage theory of development, there are two ways by which a person can adapt to an environment. These adaptation techniques are assimilation and accommodation. Together they are the causes of human development, i.e., they cause changes in cognitive structure. When an individual interacts with an environment, the new experience must be fitted into the individual's present cognitive structure. This process is known as assimilation. Sometimes a new experience is incompatible with the already existing cognitive structure and can't be fitted into it. It is then necessary for the individual to modify the individual's current cognitive structure to accommodate the new experience. The result of the two processes of assimilation and accommodation is an ever-changing cognitive structure.

Piaget assumes that the child's cognitive development passes through a series of major cognitive changes which he terms maturational stages. Such stages are postulated because of observed differences in children from one age to another. For example, Tagatz (1967) found that sixth grade subjects were less efficient than fifth grade subjects in a concept learning task. It was concluded that sixth graders were aware of the greater complexity and combinatorial aspects of the stimuli than were the fifth graders, and thus took longer to perform the conceptualizing task. This supports Piaget's contention that different stages exist in human ontogeny. It was assumed that fifth grade subjects were for the most part at a lower maturational stage than were the sixth grade subjects. If cognitive development was simply a cumulative and continuous process rather than a discontinuous process the sixth grade subjects should have been more efficient than the fifth graders.

Maturational stages are thought by Piaget to be innate in the human species. He also feels that while environmental factors may aid or hinder the process of moving from one stage to the next, the sequence of stages through which humans progress is universally the same. Piaget has identified this sequence of stages as the sensorimotor stage, preoperational stage, concrete operations stage, and formal operations stage.

Piaget's Stages of Development

Sensorimotor Stage (birth-speech)

During this stage of development from birth to the onset of speech the infant learns by means of its senses and by manipulation of objects. It is composed of six levels which describe the infant's progression from the reflexes it has at birth through the gradual modification of these reflexes as the infant interacts with its environment. In later development, the child's activities will be transformed into symbolic thought. At this stage in development, though, the child's world is a confusing one, where (1) objects have no permanency once they disappear from immediate sight, (2) objects are not distinguishable from the child as a person, and (3) time is restricted to the occurrence of a single event. In later stages when the child is able to symbolize, the world becomes more organized and acquires more meaning.

Level 1—The infant at this level of the sensorimotor stage is restricted primarily to inherited reflexive actions. The infant will reflexively respond to light and sound stimuli. If its lips are touched, the infant responds with a sucking reflex. If the mother places a rattle in the infant's palm, it will respond with a grasping reflex.

Level 2—During this level the child develops coordination for a combination of sensorimotor skills. The child can now hear and look at an object simultaneously, and then reach and grasp the object. The infant can anticipate events at this level. For instance, the infant may associate its mother carrying a bottle into the room with feeding time. The infant also exhibits a small degree of curiosity, and the ability to imitate simple behaviors of models. At this point in its development, the infant still lacks a fully mature object concept. However, when an object is removed from its visual field, it will continue to stare in the direction where the object once was.

Level 3—The infant at this level improves its object concept and ability for imitation. Now when an object disappears from sight, the infant will look for the object instead of just staring at the original location of the object. Objects now have some permanence for the infant even though they may be removed from its visual field. The infant knows that even though an object disappears out of sight, it still exists. The infant improves its ability to imitate the behavior of others; yet, it can only imitate behaviors that are familiar to it. There is also evidence that the infant is developing an ability to classify objects.

Level 4—In this level, imitative behavior develops to the extent that new behaviors can be imitated. Also the infant can imitate behaviors which it can't see itself perform. Anticipation is further developed so that the infant now expects people to behave in certain ways. Intentionality is another ability that is developed in level four. Intentionality refers to the establishment of goals, plans to meet goals, and the recognition of obstacles that must be removed in order to achieve goals. The infant's object concept continues to develop so that objects appear to have substance and permanence, and are seen as being differentiated from the infant itself.

Level 5—Sensorimotor development reaches a climactic point at this level. The child at this level is preoccupied with experimenting with new behaviors and tries out new sounds and ways of manipulating objects.

Level 6—The beginnings of symbolic thought are evident at this level. Although a model may not be physically present, the child can now construct a mental representation of a model, and then imitate its behavior. Similarly, the child is now able to mentally reconstruct the possible locations in which an object may be found, even if the object was hidden from view at the time it was placed in a particular location.

Preoperational Stage (Speech to 7 years)

The child develops language during this time, but is still unable to perform certain cognitive operations. The child uses language to symbolize, yet is still unable to group thoughts into a framework of concepts and rules. During this stage the child engages in symbolic play in which some objects stand for other objects. For example, a stick may be used as a horse, or a row of chairs may represent a passenger train. Although the ability to symbolize is evident at this stage, the child cannot mentally process a series of events.

During these years of cognitive growth, three important operations are still lacking: conservation, serialization, and class inclusion. Conservation is the realization that a property of an object remains the same although the object's physical appearance may change. For example, if a small glass filled to the top with water is emptied into a taller glass, a child who lacks the operation of volume conservation would claim that the taller glass had less water in it than the first. The child does not understand that when the physical appearance of the water was changed, its mass and volume remained the same. Serialization is the process of arranging objects in order according to some category such as weight or height. The child at the preoperational period is unable to accomplish such a task. Class inclusion is the third operation that as yet has not developed. It involves the ability to arrange parts into a whole, divide a whole into its parts, and relate parts to each other.

During the preoperational stage, the child engages in symbolic play.

The child tries to find a cause for everything at this stage, even though it may be superficial in nature. This kind of reasoning is apparent in some primitive ways of thinking exhibited at this age level. Two of these are animism and artificialism. The child who thinks in an animistic manner will attribute human characteristics such as thinking, hoping, and loving to inanimate objects. In an artificial pattern of thinking, the child will provide a coincidental explanation for the causation of some event. An example of this type of reasoning is the statement "The stars come out because the moon appears."

Several other characteristics of development can also be mentioned as being representative of children in the preoperational stage. These characteristics are egocentrism, centration, and imitation of prior events. Children at this stage think in an egocentric manner and are unable to differentiate between their thoughts and feelings and those of others. Children are able only to see things from their own perspective. Centration is the process whereby children will fix their attention upon only the most striking characteristic of an object or event. Given a choice of a black, white, or red ball, children may choose the red ball because of its color, and give no thought as to what kind of ball they wish to play with, i.e., football, basketball or baseball. Although imitation is a characteristic of the sensorimotor period, it improves during the preoperational period. Children can now imitate actions performed hours previous to the imitative act.

Concrete Operations Stage (7-11 years)

Within this stage the child's ability to think in a logical fashion develops tremendously. The child no longer relies on a trial-and-error method of problem solving, but uses a systematic method of reasoning. The child can view a particular problem from several different angles, and explore a number of solutions to a single problem. The child can reason about concrete things observed in everyday life, but is still unable to think abstractly or make hypotheses.

Children at this stage are different from what they were in previous stages because of their lack of egocentricity, their ability to classify objects, and their conception of time. Children no longer see their world in an egocentric way. They are capable of looking at a situation from another's point of view. Children at this stage can also detect multiple similarities and differences among objects and can classify them accordingly. Perception of time is no longer restricted to the time span of a single event, but it now encompasses the past as well as the present.

During these years the ability to use concrete operations is achieved. Conservation, serialization, class inclusion, and reversibility are present. Because of this understanding of conservation, the child now realizes that the mass and volume of an object remain constant even though the external appearances of the object may change. The child also possesses the ability to arrange objects in a hierarchical order according to weight, height, or some other factor. This operation was referred to previously as serialization. Class inclusion is another operation occurring during these years. The child can now form relationships between parts and wholes, and parts and other parts. Between approximately seven and eleven years of age, the child is able to reverse any logical operation to its starting point. For example, children may reason that if they had all of the balls from a playbox, besides all of the trucks they had taken from it, they would have all of the toys in the playbox. If the operation was reversed and the balls were taken away, children would be back at the original point with only the trucks from the toy box. This operation of reversibility is necessary for arithmetic reasoning.

Formal Operations Stage (11 years through adulthood)

Children in the formal operations stage no longer restrict their reasoning to concrete events. They are now capable of abstract thought and reasoning. They reflect upon their own thoughts and establish ideals for themselves. At this stage, children begin to think about the future. The distant past also assumes meaning for them. They can make hypotheses and test their veracity. This hypothetical-deductive approach to reasoning is one of the major characteristics of the formal operations stage.

With this improved problem-solving ability, children can look at a single problem from many different abstract perspectives and suggest several possible solutions. They begin to develop an organized system of rules that they can employ in their problem-solving tasks.

The formal operations stage is a product of both heredity and environmental factors. Piaget believes that by the time of puberty, the neurological basis for future cognitive growth has been laid. However, these neurological structures necessary for cognitive development continue to be influenced by environmental factors such as education, family, and peers. Thus Piaget's stage theory of cognitive development is clearly representative of an interactionist point of view.

Theoretical Approach of Jerome Bruner

Jerome Bruner proposes a different type of stage theory from Piaget to describe cognitive development (Bruner 1966). Whereas Piaget emphasizes changes in cognitive structure as children move from stage to stage, Bruner emphasizes additions to cognitive structure which children acquire as they move from the enactive mode to the ikonic mode to the symbolic mode. Bruner also emphasizes the importance of language in cognitive development as contrasted with the epistemological stage theory of Piaget which emphasizes the individual's use of logic.

Bruner's theory of cognitive development is a theory of categorizing. According to Bruner (1966), human cognitive activity requires various categorizing processes. Information processing, learning, perception, and decision making all necessitate the formation of categories. The process of categorizing allows individuals to take input from their environment and organize it in a meaningful way. Bruner claims that people are probably unable to process totally new stimuli, or at least unable to communicate the results of their processing, since the processing of stimuli relies on preexisting categories.

Categories can be thought of as rules that dictate which objects, events, or people can be grouped together on the basis of their similarities. A category tells what attributes are essential for an object to be classified in a certain group, and how the attributes must fit together. For example, the category of 'house' tells us that in order for something to be a house it must have certain attributes such as wood, brick, plaster, and nails, and that these things must be put together in a certain prescribed fashion. A category also indicates what attributes a member of a category may have, but does not necessarily have to possess. A category also sets rules governing the extent to which attributes, such as color, can vary from one situation to another, while allowing the object to maintain its membership in a particular group.

Two kinds of categories are mentioned in Bruner's theory of cognitive development: identity categories and equivalence categories. When stimuli are viewed as different forms of the same thing, the identity category is operative. An example of an identity category is a tree without its leaves in the winter, and the same tree with its leaves in the summer. Equivalence categories are employed when different objects or events are seen as being similar. Equivalence categories can be divided into three types: (1) affective, (2) functional, and (3) formal. An affective category is based on the similar emotional response that two different objects or events may arouse. When two different objects are grouped together because they share a common purpose or use, the result is a functional category. Formal categories are determined according to "convention, by law, or by science" (LeFrancois 1972). For example, the formal category for a book is determined by its dictionary definition.

A group of related categories is known as a coding system. The concept of a coding system is an important feature of Bruner's theory. By means of a coding system, categories do not remain in isolation from one another, but are related to one another in a hierarchical fashion. In proceeding from the top of the hierarchy to the bottom, one moves from the generic to the more specific. Figure 3.1 is an example of a coding system.

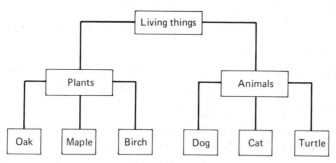

Fig. 3.1   Example of Bruner's coding system.

The acquisition of generic codes depends upon four factors: set, need state, mastery of specifics, and diversity of training. Set refers to an attitude or predisposition to react to a situation in a given way. Set can affect responding, learning, and perception. Need state refers to an individual's arousal level. Generic codes are acquired best at a moderate level of arousal. In order to set up a coding system, the individual must have sufficient knowledge about the specifics that fall under the general headings of the system. Diversity of training refers to Bruner's belief that if something is experienced under a diverse set of situations, it will relate more easily to another event.

Another concept that is central to Bruner's theory of cognitive development is language. For Bruner, language is an instrument of thought. It frees individuals from the concrete, and allows them to engage in higher, more abstract thought processes. Language is categorical, hierarchical, and grammatical. Language is categorical because words correspond to classes of things that are determined by rules or categories. These classes of objects and events are arranged hierarchically from the general to the specific. Language is grammatical because every language has a set of rules, or grammar, for governing sentence structure, and generating new combinations of words.

Assumptions of Bruner's Theory

A basic assumption in Bruner's stage theory is the interaction of heredity and environment in cognitive development. Bruner claims that neurological structures responsible for cognitive growth are inherited, but can be influenced by environmental factors such as education, family, and peers.

Other assumptions underlying Bruner's theory of cognitive development are summarized by Bruner (1966) himself in the following statements:

1. Growth is characterized by increasing independence of response from the immediate nature of the stimulus.

2. Growth depends upon internalizing events into a 'storage system' that corresponds to the environment.

3. Intellectual growth involves an increasing capacity to say to oneself and others, by means of words or symbols, what one has done or what one will do.

4. Intellectual development depends upon a systematic and contingent interaction between a tutor and a learner.

5. Teaching is vastly facilitated by the medium of language, which ends by being not only the medium for exchange but the instrument that the learner can then use himself in bringing order into the environment.

6. Intellectual development is marked by increasing capacity to deal with several alternatives simultaneously, to tend to several sequences during the same period of time, and to allocate time and attention in a manner appropriate to these multiple demands.

Bruner's Modes of Representation

Enactive

In the first year or two of life, the infant's mode of representing the world depends on action. The infant's actions give meaning to the objects around it. This early pairing of actions with objects provides the foundation for later, more complex modes of representing the world which depend less on immediate stimuli.

Ikonic

Toward the second year of life, the infant begins to represent the world in a way that is more independent of its actions. This second mode of representation employs images. In the ikonic stage of representation, the infant focuses on the surface features of objects rather than the more abstract characteristics of objects, in order to form images of them. Memories of visual experiences are restricted to the concrete and specific. However, the infant is no longer confined to the present moment in which it acts upon the environment in order to give it meaning. It is now possible for the infant to reproduce an experience through the use of images. An image is more than a mere reproduction, for it consists of the prominent characteristics of a particular experience which are arranged in a meaningful way. Images are the first cognitive units to appear. Symbols, concepts and rules are cognitive units that will develop later.

Symbolic

The symbolic stage is the highest level of abstraction that can be achieved in representing experiences. Symbolization is the process of attributing names to objects. It involves a greater degree of abstraction than imagery because, although symbols represent the objects themselves, they also point to deeper meanings not immediately apparent on the surface. For example, the symbol of the word 'flag' represents a piece of cloth with certain colors and figures on it that is flown in different countries. However, the word 'flag' also brings to

The symbolic stage is the highest level of abstraction that can be achieved in representing experiences.

mind more abstract thoughts of patriotism, motherland, and loyalty to one's country.

Language is the most important symbolic activity at this time. Through language, the child is able to reason in a logical fashion, solve complex problems, and analyze possible alternatives in various situations. Language is now the primary instrument in organizing experiences and giving meaning to them.

Piaget and Bruner Compared

The cognitive stage theories of both Piaget and Bruner are very similar, but differ in several important ways. Piaget's approach is primarily an epistemological one. He is concerned with what knowledge consists of at the different stages of development. Bruner, however, is mainly interested in the process of learning. He attempts to answer the question "How does learning take place?" While Piaget emphasizes the role of logic in learning, Bruner stresses the importance of language. Both learning theorists maintain an interactionist viewpoint, for they see learning as the product of both heredity and environment.

Although Piaget and Bruner are stage theorists, their theories differ in the number and nature of the stages. According to Piaget's theory, there are four sequential stages in cognitive development: sensorimotor, preoperational, concrete operations, and formal operations. Individuals must acquire the abilities and skills of the first stage before they can move into the next, and so on. Children can deal only with situations on the cognitive level that they have achieved at the time. Movement from one stage to the next is a result of innately regulated maturation and experience. In Bruner's theory, there are only three stages of cognitive development: enactive, ikonic, and symbolic. Bruner's enactive stage is similar to Piaget's sensorimotor period since there is a lack of object constancy and great dependence on action in both. The formal operations period in Piaget's theory and the symbolic stage of Bruner's theory are likewise comparable. In both theories, these stages represent the highest levels of cognitive development and emphasize the development of language. However, Bruner's stages are not sequential like Piaget's. According to Bruner, individuals do not necessarily proceed through an ordered set of stages, but use the stage or stages which are the most efficient in helping them to accomplish a specific task. Bruner maintains that people change from one stage to another as a result of learning and discovery, rather than from the interaction of maturation and experience. Bruner emphasizes the abilities and skills that children possess at the different stages, while Piaget stresses children's limitations at each stage.

Piaget's and Bruner's theories also differ in the implications that they have for education. Piaget believes that children should be taught only what they can deal with at their present stage in development. The instructional method employed should take into consideration the abilities and skills already acquired. Bruner, however, maintains that instruction should be directed to all three cognitive modes. The discovery approach, according to Bruner, is a preferred teaching technique.

CUMULATIVE LEARNING THEORIES OF DEVELOPMENT

Assumptions of Cumulative Learning Theory

Cumulative learning approaches to cognitive development view cognitive growth primarily as a result of learning. Unlike stage theorists such as Bruner and Piaget, cumulative learning theorists give little emphasis to maturational readiness and cognitive adaptation in their theories.

Learning occurs in a building-block manner. It is a continuous building and organizing of stimulus-response connections into more meaningful and complex systems. Once simple bonds have been made, the learning derived from these bonds can be transferred to other situations, laying the groundwork for more complex learning which involves concepts, rules, and problem solving. Cumulative learning theorists maintain that the latter types of learning cannot be mastered until the necessary prerequisite stimulus-response associations have been made. For the cumulative learning theorists, then, the whole of what is learned is merely the sum of its parts.

The essential elements in the cumulative learning approaches to cognitive development are learning, memory, and transfer. New learning, according to these approaches, occurs through the "combining of previously acquired and recalled learned entities, as well as upon their potentialities for transfer of learning" (Gagne 1968). Therefore, if a student is unable to grasp a particular concept or rule, it is because of not being adequately taught the prerequisite skills for that concept or rule. As a result, rate of cognitive development does not depend on innate factors or maturational readiness, but on the mastery of simpler prerequisite skills and habits.

Robert Gagne

One proponent of the cumulative learning approach to cognitive development is Robert Gagne. As other proponents of this approach, Gagne believes that the influence of learning on cognitive development is cumulative in its effects. Complex learning is dependent upon previous learning of simpler abilities.

Gagne, unlike some theorists, believes that all learning cannot be explained by just one theory. Gagne believes that there are eight different types of learning: signal, stimulus-response, chaining (motor chains), chaining (verbal associations), discrimination, concept, rule, and problem solving. These can be arranged in a hierarchical fashion from the simplest kind of learning, signal learning, to the most complex kind of learning, problem solving.

Each type of learning can be distinguished from the others by the conditions necessary for that type of learning to occur. These conditions are of two varieties: external and internal. External conditions refer to the learning situation itself, and how it can affect learning. Internal conditions refer to those factors characteristic of the individual learner, such as intelligence, that affect learning. The single most important condition of learning is the prerequisites that are necessary for a particular kind of learning. For example, concept learning can be distinguished from other types of learning by its prerequisites: signal learning, stimulus-response learning, chaining (motor chains), chaining (verbal associations), and discrimination learning. In other words, each level of learning is reached through the recall and transfer of knowledge, concepts, and skills obtained from the simpler types of learning that precede it.

In order for this cumulative learning to take place, previous knowledge and skills must be transferable to new situations. According to Gagne, there are two kinds of transfer in learning: lateral and vertical. In lateral transfer, the knowledge and capabilities that a learner possesses in one area can be carried over into a very similar, related area. When vertical transfer occurs, however, the knowledge and skills obtained in a certain area at one level of learning are applied in learning related subject matter that requires a more complex type of learning.

The remainder of this section will be devoted to describing each type of learning in Gagne's cumulative learning model and the conditions necessary for each type.

Signal Learning

This type of learning refers to the classical conditioning model described by Pavlov (1927). In this model, a dog learns to salivate at the sound of a bell after the bell has become associated with the presence of food. This is an involuntary response (salivation) to a conditioned stimulus (bell). The food can automatically cause salivation and, therefore, is referred to as the unconditioned stimulus. The responses made by the individual to a stimulus, or signal, in this type of learning are usually involuntary in nature, and are "general, diffuse, and emotional responses" (Gagne 1965).

The conditions necessary for signal learning are the same conditions necessary for classical conditioning. The conditioned stimulus must be presented simultaneously, or almost simultaneously, with the unconditioned stimulus in order that an association can be made between the two.

Stimulus-response Learning

This type of learning is also known as operant conditioning. Unlike signal learning, stimulus-response learning is dependent upon the individual making a specific voluntary response when a stimulus is presented. This type of response involves the use of the skeletal muscles rather than the glands as in the reflexive kinds of responses in signal-learning. An example of this type of learning is the bar pressing of a rat at the flash of a light in order to obtain food.

There are three principle conditions necessary for stimulus-response learning. First, a number of different trials must be allowed for learning to take place. Second, in order to achieve the exact response desired, the subject's behavior must be shaped by rewarding approximations of the desired behavior. Third, reward or reinforcement is essential for stimulus-response learning.

Chaining (Motor)

This third kind of learning involves chaining together previously formed stimulus-response bonds. To illustrate motor chaining, an example of a drowning child can be used. The drowning child may be a stimulus for an observer to respond by moving toward the child with the intent of rescuing him. This rescue response may act as a stimulus itself if it reminds the observer of a previous rescue attempt which almost ended fatally for him. If this is the case, the rescuer may change his mind, and respond in fear by fleeing from the scene.

This type of learning necessitates that the separate bonds within the chain be previously formed. Each link in the chain must have contiguity with the next. Motor chaining can occur in a single instance, unlike stimulus-response learning which is a gradual process.

Chaining (Verbal Association)

Verbal chaining refers to the process of linking together a series of verbal expressions that represent certain physical stimuli. This is the type of learning involved in translating words from one language into another. The conditions necessary for verbal chaining are the same as those for motor chaining.

Multiple Discrimination

In multiple discrimination learning, an individual learns to discriminate or distinguish between a set of stimuli that may resemble one another in varying degrees, and to respond to each stimulus accordingly. Discrimination learning is the kind of learning used by the young child who is beginning to identify various objects, places, and events. It is the kind of learning that takes place when names become associated with particular people.

In order for multiple discrimination to occur, two conditions are necessary. First, the differences between certain stimuli and the differences between certain responses must have been previously learned. The only thing that remains to be done in multiple discrimination is the association of the discriminated stimuli with their appropriate responses. Second, in order to prevent forgetting, precautions must be taken to eliminate interference when the associations are being established.

Concept Learning

Concept learning is the kind of learning employed in classifying stimuli according to abstract properties. It is the type of learning which allows individuals to represent their experiences in an organized and meaningful way. Two principle conditions are essential for concept learning. First, the stimulus and response portions of each chain must have been previously learned. Second, a number of different situations must be encountered in which various stimuli having the same property that is being discriminated are presented. Because of this, concept learning is often a gradual process.

Principle Learning

This type of learning results from chaining together two or more concepts. A principle expresses a relationship that exists between these concepts, and indicates what behavior should occur in certain situations. In general terms, a principle takes the form of: If X, then Y. For example, in rules of grammar, an operative principle is: If the subject of a sentence is plural, then the verb must also be plural in form.

In order for concept learning to take place, the concepts which are being associated must have been learned prior to the present learning situation. The principle can be taught verbally if the concepts have already been learned. If these conditions are met, then learning can take place on a single occasion rather than gradually.

Problem Solving

This is the highest, most complex type of learning. It is a process in which principles, previously learned, are linked together to obtain "higher-order rules." It is commonly thought of as the internal process of thinking.

There are several conditions essential for problem solving. First, the individual must recall learned principles. Second, the individual must combine these principles to formulate higher-order rules. Third, enough time must be allowed for problem solving to occur, for it may occur gradually. However, it seems that a response in a problem-solving task usually occurs in a single instance after the gradual process of combining principles is accomplished. Lastly, the individual must be aware of the characteristics of the kind of response that can solve a particular problem prior to actually deciding upon a solution.

B. F. Skinner

The behaviorist conception of learning posited by B. F. Skinner is also representative of cumulative learning theory. Unlike Gagne's model which includes eight different kinds of learning, Skinner's system classifies learning into two kinds only. He recognizes the existence of signal learning, i.e., classical conditioning, but he believes that the majority of human learning conforms to a paradigm which he calls operant conditioning.

Unlike respondent or classical conditioning, operant conditioning is a process that involves the use of voluntary muscles rather than involuntary muscles as in classical conditioning. In this type of learning, individuals must act upon their environment in order to get reinforcement. Because of this fact, operant conditioning is sometimes referred to as instrumental conditioning since individuals are instrumental in attaining reinforcement. The fact that individuals act upon their environment implies that behavior is emitted from organisms rather than elicited as in classical or respondent conditioning. In classical conditioning the association is between a stimulus and an elicited response. In operant conditioning the association is between the emitted behavior and the reinforcement upon which the behavior is contingent. These associations are cumulative in the life of a learner; and hence, Skinner's system is a cumulative-learning theory.

According to Skinner concepts such as "goals," or "desires" are not necessary for understanding how learning occurs. Equally irrelevant are constructs such as "thinking," "knowing," and "understanding." Learning is simply the result of reinforcement of behavior being emitted by an organism. Behavior which is reinforced has an increased probability of being emitted by the organism at a future time.

Basically, there are two principle processes involved in operant

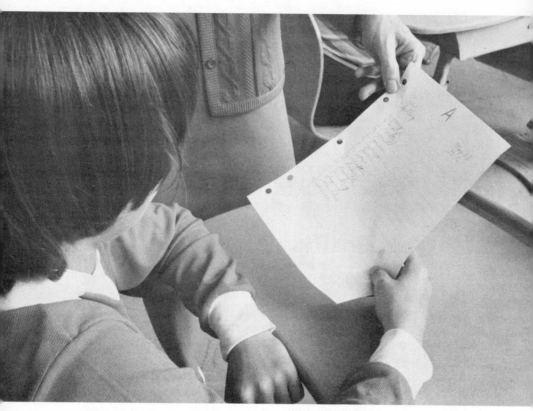

For Skinner, learning is largely the result of reinforcement.

conditioning: (1) stimulus discrimination, and (2) response differentiation. Stimulus discrimination occurs when certain behavior is emitted by a learner upon presentation of a given stimulus which either precedes that behavior or is presented simultaneously with that behavior. Stimulus discrimination then is the process whereby an organism responds in a specific manner when exposed to a certain stimulus. It is important to note that the discriminated stimulus does not elicit the response: it is merely the occasion for the organism to emit the response. Response differentiation, on the other hand, involves the modification of an original response through successive variations to a degree that meets the criterion established by the person controlling the reinforcement. Such modification of a response is called shaping. Thus the two processes both involve modification of operant behavior.

In stimulus discrimination, control can be gained over a response in terms of the situation in which a response will be emitted. In response differentiation, control can be gained directly over the nature of the response that is emitted. For example, a young boy upon entering school is aggressive in his encounters with his peers. He soon learns through differential reinforcement or aversive control that this is not appropriate behavior *in the presence of his teacher.* His behavior may stay the same in the absence of his teacher. This is an example of stimulus discrimination. Instead of providing differential reinforcement or aversive control the teacher may modify the boy's aggressive behavior through shaping. Perhaps the direction of the aggression is the modification desired by his teacher. The teacher may shape the boy's behavior from aggression directed at his peers to aggression directed at a punching bag. This is an example of response differentiation. In both instances behavior change results because of contingencies of reinforcement. In the first instance the boy's behavior changed in the presence of his teacher, and in the second instance his behavior toward his peers changed. Through the processes of response differentiation and stimulus discrimination pupils' behavior can be controlled or modified provided that appropriate reinforcement is used.

The primary principle of operant conditioning is that behavior must occur before it can be reinforced. Reinforcement of the operant response then is necessary for operant conditioning to occur. Any stimulus which increases the probability that a particular response will reoccur is referred to as a reinforcer. There are two categories of reinforcers: positive and negative. "A positive reinforcer is a stimulus which, when added to a situation, strengthens the probability of an operant response." (Hilgard 1956) Food, water, and sexual contact are examples of positive reinforcers. "A negative reinforcer is a stimulus which, when removed from a situation, strengthens the probability of an operant response." (Hilgard 1956) Negative reinforcers are aversive stimuli and include such things as loud noise, very bright light, and extreme heat or cold. The effect of reinforcement, either positive or negative, is an increased probability that the response will be emitted.

Positive and negative reinforcers can be further classified as to whether they are primary reinforcers or secondary reinforcers. A primary reinforcer is a stimulus that is naturally reinforcing to an organism. Examples of primary reinforcers are food, water, and sexual contact. A secondary reinforcer is any stimulus which when paired with a primary reinforcer becomes reinforcing in itself. Secondary reinforcers are important in Skinner's system because of their ability to be generalized. A secondary reinforcer is generalized when it is paired with more than one primary reinforcer (Skinner 1953). Money is a convenient illustration of a positive secondary reinforcer, because money provides access to primary reinforcers. It is thus a generalized reinforcer. Secondary reinforcers become generalized through repeated association with either primary reinforcers or other secondary reinforcers. This generalization of reinforcers is analogous to Pavlov's classical conditioning.

It is possible to employ different schedules of reinforcement in order to meet the circumstances and the desired results. Schedules of reinforcement play a very important role in learning since the frequency of reinforcement, the time lapse between reinforcements, and the variability or fixedness of a particular schedule strongly effect learning, forgetting, and extinction. There are two main types of reinforcement schedules: nonintermittent, and intermittent. Nonintermittent schedules include continuous schedules where every response is reinforced, and extinction schedules, where no response is reinforced. Intermittent schedules fall into four groups: (1) fixed interval, (2) fixed ratio, (3) variable interval, and (4) variable ratio. In a fixed interval schedule, reinforcement is given only after a set time interval, e.g., every 30 seconds, while in a fixed ratio schedule, reinforcement is given after a fixed number of responses, e.g., every fifth response. In a variable interval schedule, reinforcement is not given at a fixed time interval, but is based on an average time interval. For example reinforcement may be given, on the average, every 30 seconds, but the interval between each reinforcement may vary from a few seconds to several minutes. In a variable ratio schedule, reinforcement is not given after a fixed number of responses, but is based on an average number of responses. For instance, reinforcement may be given, on the average, every sixth response, but the number of responses emitted between reinforcements may vary from none to twelve or more.

Extinction is the process whereby reinforcement for certain behavior is no longer given. Once reinforcement is withdrawn, the likelihood of the behavior being emitted decreases. According to Skinner (1953) the extinction curve, which indicates how quickly certain behavior stops after reinforcement is no longer given, is a good means of assessing the effect of the reinforcement. His findings indicate that intermittent reinforcement gives the best results over a long period of time. Extinction is an effective method of ridding an organism's behavior repertoire of certain undesired habits. Sometimes, even though reinforcement has been withdrawn for certain behaviors, they may reappear for a short time before they disappear permanently. This phenomenon is known as spontaneous recovery.

Punishment should not be confused with reinforcement. While reinforcement increases the probability that a response will recur, punishment merely decreases the probability that an undesired response will occur in a particular situation. Punishment is the presentation of a noxious stimulus or the removal of a positive stimulus after a response has occurred. Reinforcement, on the other hand, is the withdrawal of a noxious stimulus, or the presentation of a positive one after a response has occurred. Punishment merely suppresses a response, but does not extinguish it.

COMPARISON OF CUMULATIVE LEARNING AND STAGE THEORIES

The four theorists discussed in this chapter are representative of the two main divisions in theories of cognitive development: stage theories and cumulative learning theories. For stage theorists, the formation of and changes in cognitive structures and the way that individuals perceive and organize their environment are essential aspects to an understanding of both learning and cognitive development. Cumulative learning theorists, however, emphasize the importance of forming associations or bonds. For them, cognitive development is primarily, if not solely, a process of building up simple associations into more complex configurations. The stage theorists disagree with this viewpoint, explaining that learning is a process which involves the understanding of relationships and the organization of sensory experiences. The stage theorists also stress the importance of insight in learning, whereas cumulative learning theorists give little or no recognition to such variables that intervene between a stimulus and response.

Hilgard and Bower (1966) claim that the two different groups of theorists differ in three principal ways: (1) peripheral versus central intermediaries, (2) acquisition of habits versus acquisition of cognitive structures, and (3) trial-and-error versus insight in problem solving. In goal-seeking situations, the cognitive stage theorists would maintain that central intermediaries, such as memories or hypotheses, are involved. However, cumulative learning theorists would emphasize peripheral intermediaries such as muscular responses. For example, cumulative learning theorists claim that an organism moves toward a goal, not because of the influence of certain memories or expectations, but because of chained muscular responses. The second difference between the two theoretical positions is their definition of learning. For stage theorists, learning is the forming and changing of cognitive structures. To the cumulative learning theorists, learning is primarily, and sometimes solely, the acquisition of habits. The third difference between stage and cumulative learning theorists is their answers to how an individual arrives at a solution to a new problem. The cumulative learning theorists claim that learning from past situations is transferred to new, similar situations. If transfer is not possible, the learner resorts to the trial-and-error method of solving a problem. Stage theorists agree with these techniques of problem solving, but also add insight as another possible way of solving a problem.

While these three differences relate primarily to explanations of learning from the two theoretical positions, they serve to illustrate the differences in theories of cognitive development as perceived from each position. Cognitive development from the cumulative learning theory position results exclusively from the prior experiences which the learner has had. Such experiences result in responses and modifications of responses. The human organism is viewed as the sum or total of the responses it is capable of making. If experience has this importance, then the logical implication for education of this position is to control the learner's environment as completely as possible. This will assure that the learner has the "right" experiences and will therefore make the "right" responses. The learner will have the "right" cognitive development.

Stage theorists view cognitive development as a more complex phenomenon than do the cumulative learning theorists. Not only is cognitive development a function of experiences but it is also governed by hereditary factors. The human organism is viewed as having an innate need to interact with its environment and has innate changes in its ability to reason or use sensory modalities. The logical implications for education of this position are almost antithetical to the cumulative learning position. They suggest that the learner be involved in goal-setting activities in which decisions are made as to what should next be experienced.

STIMULATING COGNITIVE DEVELOPMENT THROUGH INDIVIDUALLY GUIDED EDUCATION

Implications of Stage Theories

According to Piaget's theory, a teacher should be aware of the developmental stage at which each child is functioning, and each should be taught only what the child is ready to learn at the present stage of development. According to this theory, teachers may be detrimental to learning if they do not recognize that children reach stages of cognitive development at different chronological ages and teach accordingly. For example, the curriculum should be planned with the level of cognitive operations and structures that children have successfully attained in mind. Teachers should act as guides, working with each child as the child interacts with the environment, ensuring that experiences are appropriate for the developmental stage at which the child is functioning.

Bruner agrees that the teacher should be a guide in the educational process. In addition, he maintains that instruction should be directed toward all three cognitive levels since the individual relies on whichever one is the most efficient in a given instance. He further states that students should often be exposed to a discovery approach to learning so that autonomy and self-direction will be learned.

Unlike Piaget who emphasizes differences in cognitive growth rate but the universality of stages, Bruner places considerable emphasis on individual differences in cognitive development and cognitive learning styles of students. What Bruner says about individual differences is important for education, especially for those involved with individualized programs of instruction.

In addition to differences in the students' cognitive level in a particular situation, Bruner's theory encompasses individual differences in terms of the conditions that affect an individual's acquisition of a skill, and the strategies that different individuals may employ in concept attainment. Bruner maintains that people differ with respect to their needs, their sets toward particular tasks, the degree to which they've mastered specific knowledge which is prerequisite for the acquisition of a particular skill, and the diversity of their previous learning situations. According to Bruner, individuals also differ in the types of strategies they use in arriving at a particular concept. Usually, individuals tend to have a predominant conceptual strategy, and teachers should be cognizant of which one is utilized by each student. Thus teachers should be aware of all sources of difference among individuals since the sources cause variations in children's patterns of cognitive development.

Implications of Cumulative Learning Theories

In Gagne's cumulative learning theory, emphasis is placed on learning, rather than maturational readiness, in cognitive development. Learning is not so much dependent on hereditary factors as it is on the acquisition of necessary skills. Gagne believes that the school can increase the rate of an individual's cognitive development. The more skills that a teacher teaches, and the faster the teacher does this, the more quickly a child will progress in cognitive development. Gagne believes that an educational program should be self-paced since some students will lack necessary prerequisite skills and will have to acquire these before they can move ahead. Other students will be far more advanced in their acquisition of various skills and can progress at a much faster rate.

When new concepts are being taught, the teacher should follow Gagne's eight levels of learning, proceeding from the simplest to the more complex kinds of learning. This could be accomplished by dividing a concept to be learned into various elements and organizing them according to their level of difficulty. The teacher can begin with the easiest elements of the concept and then advance to the more difficult elements.

Reinforcement plays a vital role in the educational process according to Skinner. When a student responds appropriately, the teacher should reinforce the student in order to increase the possibility of future appropriate responses. Various reinforcement schedules affect learning, forgetting, and extinction in different ways. The teacher should be aware of the effects of these different schedules on learning. For example, intermittent reinforcement is the best schedule for preventing extinction of learning.

Skinner's theory also suggests that an educational program should be self-paced. This is because a different number of reinforcements are necessary for habits to be established in different people, and therefore it takes some people longer to learn than others. Skinner suggests the use of programmed texts in such a self-paced program. Teaching machines are also thought by Skinner to be effective means of allowing students to learn at their own rate.

Implications of an Interactive Perspective

The soft deterministic view that it is possible for human behavior to be a function of antecedent events and also possible for people to ultimately retain their freedom helps to resolve the apparent differences between the cognitive stage theories and the cumulative learning theories discussed in this chapter. It also provides guidance as to which theories to implement when actually working with children in a school setting. Individually Guided Education provides an environment in which both theoretical viewpoints can be implemented to the benefit of individual learners. In general, cumulative learning theory should be applied when external control is required by the educational context, and stage theory should be utilized when cognitive self-control or self-direction is desired. For example, in the area of language arts external control is required during the time a child is learning to read. After the child's reading skill is developed, the skill can be used to explore books that fulfill the child's needs in the present cognitive stage, whether these books be fairy tales, science books, or history books.

Teaching machines allow students to learn at their own rate.

For example, in Jefferson County, Denver, Colorado, Bear Creek Elementary School, Joanne Vivian met with her teammates the first week in November, 1973, to discuss reading placement for students who had mastered Level A of the *Wisconsin Design for Reading Skill Development* and some of Level B. Donnie, an aggressive out-spoken first grader, was one child who had completed all of Level A and most of Level B. Donnie was independent and impatient. He needed to learn to work with the group, but he also needed freedom to do his own "thing." Donnie was grouped with other children who had mastered about the same number of reading skills as he and who were compatible with each other. Donnie's group, named the Turtles, met with Mrs. Vivian on Monday for 30 minutes. At that time group goals were discussed and new reading skills were introduced to Donnie. Oral reading and comprehension were stressed. Donnie's group used their basal reader as a springboard for individual activi-ties. After 30 minutes of group work with Mrs. Vivian, Donnie did 30 minutes of review work at his desk. An aide, Barbara Argibrite, supervised Donnie's activities and reinforced appropriate responses in his review work. The last 30 minutes Donnie went to the Instruc-tional Materials Center (IMC) with Mrs. Stricebottom. Donnie then chose what he wanted to do within a prescribed framework. In the center were three long-vowel games. Donnie, being the Turtles' cap-tain, put the games on the floor and formed groups to play the game. Donnie's favorite was "Long Vowel Lotto." Donnie, Lonnie, and Mitch played the game. When done, Donnie put the game away and decided to play with clay. Mitch chose a book and read quietly. Lonnie drew a picture about the day's story. At the end of 30 min-utes, the aide gathered the Turtles together. They talked about the independent work they had completed. Did they work well together? Did they enjoy themselves? What improvements were made? Donnie decided center activities went well.

It can be inferred that cumulative learning theory was used as the theoretical basis to continue Donnie's acquisition of the basic reading skills. In a skills group, Donnie continued work on the skills in the *Wisconsin Design for Reading Skill Development*. Twenty minutes a day Donnie was given instruction on a reading skill he had not mastered. At the end of each skill program, Donnie was given a test. Donnie passed the test on blends with 90 percent mas-tery. He was then able to give his attention to another skill. In his reading group, Donnie was given daily instruction on the skills intro-duced with that story. Donnie finished all of Level B and Level C that year and was thus an independent reader by the end of the year.

It can further be inferred that stage theory was used as the theoretical base in order to group Donnie with peers at his stage of development and to help them to acquire independence. In one instance, Mrs. Vivian used *Peter and the Wolf* to facilitate this acquisition. Donnie, given a list of possible suggestions of ways to study folktales, decided to do the following:

1. Study filmstrips on folktales.
2. Read other folktales.
3. Write his own folktale and illustrate it.
4. Join a group and put on a folktale play.

By the end of the year, Donnie was critically judging books that he had chosen to read and was giving detailed book reports, an activity students at his stage of development can normally do.

This illustration demonstrates that both cognitive stage theories and cumulative learning theories imply the need for an educational experience which is attentive to the uniqueness of the individual. Cognitive stage theories attend to volitional aspects, self-control, and direction while cumulative learning theories imply that external or environmental control can be most effective. From the soft deterministic viewpoint, both are important in individualized education.

SUGGESTED READINGS FOR CHAPTER 3

Gagne, R. M. 1968. Contributions of learning to human development. *Psychological Review* 75: 177–191.

Gagne contrasts his eight stages of cumulative learning with two other theoretical positions regarding human intellectual development—Hall and Gessell's view of growth readiness and Piaget's model (theory) of cognitive learning (development).

Flavell, J. H. 1963. *The developmental psychology of Jean Piaget*. Princeton, N.J.: Van Nostrand.

In three major sections Flavell provides a comprehensive and detailed summary of Piaget's theoretical model of human development, the experimental basis of the major features of the model, and a critique of Piaget's work, both methodologically and in view of related work done by others.

Bruner, J. S., R. R. Oliver, and P. M. Greenfield *et al.* 1966. *Studies in cognitive growth*. New York: Wiley.

The nature of cognitive growth—the attainment and use of knowledge—is treated in this book from both a theoretical and experimental perspective. The basic premise espoused by the authors is that cognitive growth is manifested as a series of psychological events, each requiring explanation in terms of psychological processes. Special emphasis is placed on the growth of three psychological systems for representing information—through action, through imagery, and through symbolism of language. This emphasis is paralleled by the view that manifestations of cognitive growth occur as much from cultural influences as from a purely maturational sequence of development.

REFERENCES

Bigge, M. L. 1971. *Learning theories for teachers.* (2nd ed.) New York: Harper & Row.

Bruner, J. S. 1966. *Toward a theory of instruction.* New York: Norton.

————, R. R. Oliver, and P. M. Greenfield *et al.* 1966. *Studies in cognitive growth.* New York: Wiley.

Communications Research Machines 1971. *Developmental psychology today.* Del Mar, Calif.

Communications Research Machines 1973. *Educational psychology: a contemporary view.* Del Mar, Calif.

Flavell, J. H. 1963. *The developmental psychology of Jean Piaget.* Princeton, N.J.: Van Nostrand.

Gagne, R. M. 1968. Contributions of learning to human development. *Psychological Review* 75: 177–191.

———— 1966. Elementary science: a new scheme of instruction. *Science Magazine* 151: January 49–53.

———— 1965. *The conditions of learning.* New York: Holt.

Garry, R. G., and H. L. Kingsley 1970. *The nature and conditions of learning.* (3rd ed.) Englewood Cliffs, N.J.: Prentice-Hall.

Ginsburg, H., and S. Opper 1969. *Piaget's theory of intellectual development: an introduction.* Englewood Cliffs, N.J.: Prentice-Hall.

Hilgard, E. R. 1962. *Introduction to psychology.* New York: Harcourt.

————, and G. H. Bower 1966. *Theories of learning.* (3rd ed.) New York: Meredith.

———— 1956. *Theories of learning.* New York: Appleton-Century-Crofts.

LeFrancois, G. R. 1972. *Psychological theories and human learning: Kongor's report.* Monterey, Calif.: Brooks/Cole.

Pavlov, I. P. 1927. *Conditioned reflexes.* London: Oxford University Press.

Phillips, J. L. 1969. *The origins of intellect: Piaget's theory.* San Francisco: Freeman.

Piaget, J. 1952. *The origins of intelligence in children.* New York: Norton.

Rohwer, W. D., Jr. 1970. Cognitive development and education. In P. H. Mussen (ed.), *Carmichael's manual of child psychology.* Vol. 1. (3rd ed.) New York: Wiley.

Skinner, B. F. 1953. *Science and human behavior.* New York: Macmillan.

Tagatz, G. E. 1967. Effects of strategy, sex, and age on conceptual behavior of elementary school children. *Journal of Educational Psychology* 58: 103–109.

4

Language Development

Objectives

Upon completion of this chapter, the reader should be able:

- To understand the relationship of phonemes, morphemes, words, sentences, syntax and semantics as components of language development.
- To identify and distinguish among the nativist, imitation-reinforcement, and rule-learning theories of language development.
- To understand the developmental sequence in the acquisition of meaning.
- To articulate ways that language development can be nurtured through Individually Guided Education.

. . . thought is a bird of space, that in a cage of words may indeed unfold its wings but cannot fly.

Kahlil Gibran*

THEORIES OF LANGUAGE DEVELOPMENT

Within the first few years of life almost all children master their language, a system of communication so unique that it is often considered one of the major factors which sets *Homo sapiens* apart from other animal species. This is not to say that animals do not communicate with one another. On the contrary, most animal species seem to have some means of communication whereby they exchange information. In many respects, the speech behavior of some animals resembles human language. The closer an animal species is to humankind on the phylogenetic scale, the more its speech behavior resembles human language. Despite the fact that some animal species have developed rather intricate systems of communication, none has been shown to possess the technology of communication called language.

Hockett (1960) states that there are several features which differentiate the human communication systems from those of animals. These features make it possible for us, creatures with limited powers of discrimination and memory, to create and comprehend an almost infinite variety of communications. One feature that is unique to human communication is termed duality of patterning, which refers to the fact that human language is structured and organized on the basis of a small number of sounds. Sounds are placed in various arrangements, or patterns, to form units of meaning. These units of meaning are then placed in various arrangements, or patterns, to form units of thought.

Descriptive linguists, in their studies of human language, have identified the various units of language and placed them in a hierarchy (Figure 4.1). Phonemes are the smallest units of sound in a language. Sounds which are symbolized by vowels, consonant-vowel, and vowel-consonant combinations, such as *e*, *le*, and *ex* in the English language, are phonemes. Even when reciting the alphabet a person uses sound combinations. The English alphabet written according to sound would begin: *a, be, ce, de, e, ef*, etc. The English alpha-

---

* Reprinted from *The prophet*, by Kahlil Gibran, with the permission of the publisher, Alfred A. Knopf, Inc. Copyright 1923 by Kahlil Gibran; renewal copyright 1951 by Administrators C.T.A. of Kahlil Gibran Estate, and Mary G. Gibran.

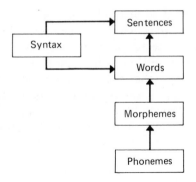

Fig. 4.1 Hierarchy of units of language.

bet does not include all the sounds of the English language. Other sounds such as *ch* and two *th*'s are also present. The English language has a total of 44 sounds. Other languages utilize sounds which are not in the English language, and some do not use sounds that are used in the English language. Thus one reason why the languages of the world are unique is because they comprise different sounds.

Morphemes compose the next unit of language identified by descriptive linguists. Morphemes are combinations of one or more phonemes and are the smallest units of meaning in a language. The endings *s* and *es* added as suffixes to English nouns are examples of morphemes. These plural suffixes add meaning to nouns; they signal the plurality of persons, places, and things.

Words are the third unit of language, and are composed of one or more morphemes. For example, *you*, *a*, and *the* are one-morpheme words. An example of a two-morpheme word is *cigarettes*. It is composed of the morpheme *cigarette* and the morpheme *s*. Both morphemes making up *cigarettes* are meaningful units. *Cigarette* specifies the object of reference and *s* indicates the plural nature of the noun.

The final unit of language is the sentence which is a special pattern of one or more words. Both *"Stop."* and *"Stop the car."* are sentences. Words and sentences, the last two units of language, are patterned by sets of rules termed syntax. For example, the syntax of the English language contains the rule that the article *a* usually precedes singular nouns which begin with a consonant and the article *an* usually precedes singular nouns which begin with a vowel sound. Syntax is another of the language components which creates differences among human languages. Only those combinations of morphemes which follow the syntax of a language yield words and sentences which are meaningful.

In order for a child to acquire a native language, the child must master the phonemic, morphemic and syntactical components as well as the meaning of the words of that language. It appears that the acquisition of meaning continues throughout an individual's life. However, the acquisition of the phonemic, morphemic, and syntactical components of the child's native language is for the most part completed by the time the child enters first grade. The developmental sequence of these language components is presented in Figure 4.2.

Age	Period	Description
0-2 months	Prelinguistic vocalization	Approximately four vowels present in noncrying vocalization
2+ months	Babbling	Consonant-vowel, vowel-consonant phonemes present
4+ months	Imitation	Imitates own speech and responds vocally to speech of others
8+ months	Repetition	Combines phonemes, e.g., lili, geegee
11+ months	First word	Combines phonemes for expression, e.g., "dada," "mama." Usually refers to concrete object and used to indicate many situations.
12+ months	Two-word vocabulary	Two words present in vocabulary
2+ years	Two-word sentences	Usually noun and verb combinations, e.g., "car go," "drink milk."
2-3 years	Syntax	Beginning of the use of grammar

Fig. 4.2 Language development sequence.

While this sequence of language development is generally accepted by developmental theorists, there exists considerable controversy as to how this development occurs. Three different theoretical approaches have been taken in attempting to explain how people develop their ability to communicate: (1) the nativistic approach, (2) the imitation-reinforcement approach, and (3) the rule-learning or rule-induction approach. Each suggests that different mechanisms, processes, and strategies occur in an individual's acquisition of language.

Nativistic Theory

Proponents of nativistic theories of language development (Chomsky, 1965; McNeill, 1966, 1970; Lenneberg, 1964; Katz, 1966) emphasize the innate ability of humans to acquire language. They postulate that children possess information about the universal aspects of language, such as the existence of *subjects, predicates, objects,* and *sentences,* as well as an inborn ability to evaluate linguistic information. These innate factors allow developing children to formulate hypotheses concerning their native languages, and to evaluate these hypotheses through their interaction with their environment. While both genetic and environmental factors are necessary for language development to occur, according to nativists, innate factors are the more important.

The role of innate factors in language development is demonstrated in the nativist language development model called a language acquisition device or LAD. Nativists believe that as children hear a language, they process the language in a way similar to this model. Chomsky (1968) and McNeill (1970) have identified two distinct components of the language acquisition device. Linguistic information, the first component, contains those aspects of human language which are universal to all human languages. Evaluation procedures make up the second component. Nativists believe language learners have a built-in mechanism which allows them to construct, test, and evaluate hypotheses concerning the structure of a particular language. Figure 4.3 illustrates the way nativists describe language development through LAD.

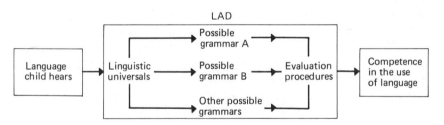

Fig. 4.3 A nativistic theory of language development.

Nativists believe that language learning is a deductive process. The evaluation component of the language acquisition device, or children's inborn ability to formulate, test, and evaluate hypotheses about language, allows them to gradually deduce the specific structure of their native languages from their knowledge of linguistic universals. Children spontaneously formulate a number of hypotheses concerning the grammatical form of the language they hear, and test these hypotheses within their linguistic environment. Those particular hypotheses that prove compatible with the language that the children hear are selected by the children as components of the grammar, or structure, of their native languages. Through this deductive process children move toward linguistic competence.

Nativists also propose that because language acquisition is a deductive process, it is an active and sequential process as well. Children are active in that they formulate, test, and evaluate hypotheses concerning the structure of their languages. The process is sequential because, as children gain knowledge about their languages, they are able to formulate, test, and evaluate new hypotheses based on that knowledge.

To substantiate their theory of language development, nativists point to certain linguistic phenomena which occur in young children. The ability of young children to acquire a great deal of linguistic competence within the first few years of life is considered evidence of the existence of innate language acquisition abilities. The ability of most young children to understand language structures which they cannot produce themselves, or to comprehend spoken language better than they can produce it, supports the existence of innate linguistic abilities. Nativists also cite the linguistic mistakes exhibited by young children as proof that children formulate, test, and evaluate linguistic hypotheses. An example of a mistake made universally by children learning language is overgeneralization of grammatical rules. Linguists have observed that young children use grammatical rules which are too general. For example, when a child first learns to use *d* or *ed* to form the past tense of verbs he applies this rule to regular and irregular verbs alike. This yields such words as *comed*, *doed*, and *breaked* which are grammatically incorrect because the rule applies to regular verbs only. Children require time to learn to restrict the rule to appropriate situations. As they narrow the application of the rule to regular verbs only, the overgeneralizations gradually disappear from their speech. Nativists contend that children are deducing the structure of their languages when they learn to restrict a rule which they initially overgeneralized.

The nativist theory of language acquisition, a process of deduction built upon innate linguistic abilities, adequately explains the fact that children who are learning language, as well as the older individual who has acquired linguistic competence, can generate unique sentences. Even the very young children can produce sentences which they have never heard or spoken before. Because they have an inborn knowledge of linguistic universals, and because they have deduced the underlying structure of the language they hear, individuals are able to create unique meaningful sentences. Individuals can also understand the speech of others even when it is imperfect. As examples, normal hesitancies, word and phrase repetitions, false starts, and so forth, usually do not interfere with listeners' ability to understand another's speech because they can deduce what the language should be.

Rule-learning Theory

Proponents of rule-learning or rule-induction theories of language development (Brown and Fraser 1964, Berko 1958, Ervin 1964) emphasize the roles of both innate and environmental factors in language acquisition. They postulate the existence of an innate processing mechanism which helps children to reach an understanding of the structure of their native languages. The language of the child's environment provides the linguistic data fed into this processing mechanism. The complementary and interdependent roles of innate and environmental factors are displayed by rule-learning models of language development. Figure 4.4 presents one such model which was

	Example
Children discover their language has forms which aid communication.	past tense
Children discover that these forms follow rules and tries to apply rules they formulate.	add *d* or *ed*
Children overgeneralize or overregularize.	*doed* or *comed*
Children discover the rules do not apply in all cases.	*doed* and *comed* are not correct
New rules are formulated and applied.	forms new rule for the past tense of *come* and *do*

Fig. 4.4 A rule-learning model of syntactical development.

suggested by Hopper and Naremore (1973) as an explanation of syntactical development. The language children hear, according to this and other rule-learning models, is an essential input from which children first discover that rules exist, then formulate, apply, and evaluate these rules. Children do not have information concerning universal aspects of language. They must discover both the universal aspects and the particular aspects of their native languages from this input. The innate processing mechanism that children possess enables them to do this. It contains a set of procedures or rules that help them to infer relationships from linguistic data.

Rule-learning theorists also believe that children acquire the structures of their languages by an inductive rather than a deductive process. Children's innate language processing device guides them from the specific, the language structure that they hear around them, to the general, or the overall structure of their native languages. Children compile specific information from what they hear and formulate hypotheses concerning the nature of this language. Children are instrumental in the language development process according to the rule-learning approach. Not only do they formulate, test, and evaluate hypotheses concerning the rules of their languages but they also actively compile linguistic information to use in the formulation of hypotheses.

Rule-learning theorists emphasize some of the same linguistic phenomena as nativists. The points they choose to stress include: the early acquisition of language; the existence of linguistic mistakes such as overgeneralization during language development; and the ability of individuals to comprehend and produce sentences which they have never heard or used before. These phenomena are explainable by the innate and environmental interaction postulated by these theorists.

Most rule-induction language theorists do not attempt to explain the exact nature of the rule-induction process. They propose that the child is furnished with an innate linguistic processing mechanism, but their knowledge and understanding of how this built-in mechanism is used by the child is incomplete. Some researchers, Braine (1965) for instance, suggest that children's induction of linguistic rules is simply stimulus-generalization learning. Braine proposes that children learn to associate words with the particular position that the words hold within sentences. By experiencing a word in a specific position in a sentence (e.g., at the end of the sentence) many times and in many contexts, children learn to use that word in the position in which they have experienced it. For example, children who say things like "boot off," "light off," "pants off" have learned to associate the word *off* with the final position in a phrase or sentence. In such sentences as "all broke," "all gone," and "all done," they have formed an association between the word *all* and the initial position. Children have not induced a positional rule to the effect that the preposition "off" follows nouns, they have simply learned to "associate" the words with the final position in a sentence. Not every word in young children's vocabulary is strongly associated with a position.

In fact, most words are not. Braine divides the words in children's vocabularies into two classes. Pivot class words are a small number of words for which a child knows the proper position, (e.g., *off*, *all*). These words are seldom used alone, but are usually used in combination with open class words. Open class words are those which are used in any number of positions. They can be used alone, in combination with other open class words, or in combination with pivot class words. Open class words make up the large part of a child's vocabulary. Pivot and open class words, if they describe a true distinction in children's vocabularies, provide a structural basis for combining and ordering words. As the child's syntactic knowledge increases, these word class distinctions develop into the complex grammar of adult language.

Imitation-reinforcement Theory

Proponents of imitation-reinforcement theories of language development (Mowrer 1960, Staats 1961 and 1968, Skinner 1957) emphasize the role of environment in language acquisition. They contend that humans have no innate knowledge of linguistic structure and no innate processing mechanism. According to these theorists, the inborn factors which enable humans to acquire language are simple learning abilities, such as the ability to form associations. Language is learned entirely through experience; the child's environment supplies a linguistic model and provides the experience necessary for language development.

Imitation-reinforcement theorists explain the acquisition of language through the principles of classical and operant conditioning (see Chapter 3). They believe that language development begins when the infant first begins to make random, experimental sounds. These early sounds are differentially reinforced by the infant's parents. As a result, sounds which are *not* phonemes of the infant's native language are gradually dropped from the infant's vocalizations; those sounds which are features of the infant's native language emerge as prominent sounds in the child's vocalizations. At the same time, the sounds made by the infant's parents which are associated with primary reinforcers become secondary reinforcers for the child (e.g., parents talking to the child during feeding). As the reinforcement value of the parents' voices increases and generalizes to the infant's own vocalizations, the sounds that the child makes become reinforcing in and of themselves. It is the direct reinforcement by the parents plus the self-reinforcement of the infant which lead to the gradual acquisition of sounds, syllables, and finally words according to imitation-reinforcement theorists.

Once a repertoire of words has been established, the child begins to combine them. Some imitation-reinforcement theorists (Staats, 1961, 1968) believe that the child's ability to make word combinations depends upon the behavior of the parents. They contend that parents expand a child's single-word responses into sentences, withholding reinforcement until the child imitates the expansion. For example, single words spoken by the child such as *cookie* and *milk* are expanded by parents to "cookie please" and "milk please"; the milk or cookie is withheld until some approximation of these two-word expansions is provided by the child. Thus the parental expansion becomes a discriminative stimulus. The child learns to expand the speech in the presence of this stimulus to gain reinforcement. Figure 4.5 illustrates this expansion process. The expansion is instrumental in the acquisition of word combinations of all lengths.

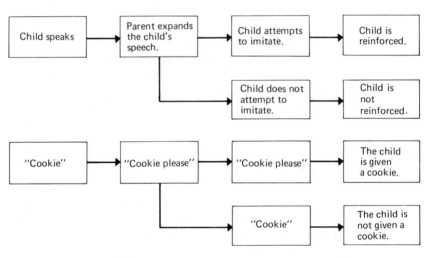

Fig. 4.5   An example of expansion.

As children hear the language of their environment, they gradually acquire knowledge of the relationships among words in sentences. For example, the child hears sentences like "Buy the bread," "Eat the food," and "Drive the car," and learns the conditions when *the* occurs; between *buy* and *bread* when a person wants a specific type of bread, between *eat* and *food* when a person wants specific food eaten, and so forth. Also words which occur after *the* children learn to associate through conditioning with the word *the*. They learn that *the* appears before nouns and adjectives, but not pronouns, verbs or adverbs. Eventually, more and more words become interconnected in increasingly complex arrangements. Children hear and learn only those word combinations which are exhibited in the language they are learning. For example, *the* is not placed before such words as *there* and *because* in the English language, so combinations like *the there* and *the because* do not develop in the speech of English-speaking children. Imitation-reinforcement theorists claim that a conditioning process accounts for the child's acquisition both of phrases and whole sentences.

Imitation-reinforcement theorists differ from nativists and rule-learning theorists in the linguistic phenomena they choose to emphasize. They stress the sequence of language development and specific aspects of child-environment relationships, such as the language present in a child's environment, the reinforcement the child receives for attempting to communicate, the expansion of the child's communication by parents, and the imitation of heard communications by children.

AN ANALYSIS OF THE LANGUAGE DEVELOPMENT THEORIES

One comparison that can be made among the three language development theories is with respect to the emphasis given to innate and environmental factors; differing amounts and types of innate abilities are postulated in each of the three theories. Nativist theorists place primary emphasis on innate factors. They state that the child has inborn knowledge concerning the universal aspects of language as well as a mechanism for evaluating the specific language of the environment. Rule-learning theorists place approximately equal emphasis upon innate and environmental factors. Children have innate language-processing abilities which help them to evaluate their native language according to rule-learning theorists. Imitation-reinforcement theorists emphasize environmental influences in the language learning process. Children learn language through conditioning. The only innate abilities recognized by imitation-reinforcement theorists are general learning abilities. The three language acquisition theories may be viewed as illustrating three different positions on the nature-nurture question: nativists favor nature, imitation-reinforcement theorists favor nurture, and rule-learning theorists favor a middle position.

A second comparison that can be made among the three language development theories is with respect to their perception of a person's relationship with the environment. Developmental theorists view humans as either organisms interacting with their environment or organisms which are being acted upon by their environment. Nativistic and rule-learning theories perceive children as actively involved in language acquisition. They believe children are active in selecting, testing, and utilizing processes for evaluating linguistic hypotheses. Rule-learning theorists see children as active in formulating, testing, and evaluating linguistic hypotheses. Imitation-reinforcement theorists view children as the passive recipients of language; that is, they learn language through conditioning. Children do not choose, but rather respond to environmental stimuli and are reinforced for responding correctly. Imitation-reinforcement theorists, by viewing humans as passively involved with their environment, differ from other language development theorists who view humans as active agents in their environment.

A third comparison that can be made among the three theories refers to the nature of the cognitive processes involved in language acquisition. Nativists view language acquisition as a deductive process in which children deduce the rules governing the language they hear from the information they have on the universal aspects of language. Rule-learning theorists describe language acquisition as an inductive process; children induce the structure of their language from the specific language samples they hear. Imitation-reinforcement theorists reject the idea that children either induce or deduce linguistic rules when they first learn to communicate. Rather, imitation-reinforcement theorists view language acquisition as a conditioning process; children gradually learn specific associations, specific discriminations, and specific responses. Nativists and rule-learning theorists, then, view the acquisition of rules as an integral part of language development. They differ in that nativists view rule acquisition as a deductive process while rule-learning theorists view it as an inductive one. Imitation-reinforcement theorists do not accept the acquisition of rules as part of initial language development. They explain language acquisition through the process of conditioning.

The final comparison is based upon the particular facets of language upon which theorists choose to focus. Linguists traditionally have drawn a distinction between linguistic performance and linguistic competence. Linguistic performance refers to the actual acts of speaking and hearing, and linguistic competence refers to speaker-listeners' knowledge of the sound patterns, syntax and semantics underlying their language performance. Nativists and rule-learning theorists, who look upon language as an abstract system of organizing principles which underlies the actual speech acts, focus their research upon linguistic competence. They believe that the innovative aspects of an individual's language, or an ability to generate and understand novel sentences, can be accounted for only by linguistic competence. Nativists and rule-learning theorists try to discover which underlying rules or principles of language a child has mastered and put to use in linguistic performance. Imitation-reinforcement theories, which argue that language is a set of behavioral responses acquired in the presence of particular stimuli, are theories of linguistic performance. Imitation-reinforcement theorists focus their research upon the individual's actual speech output, as flawed as it is by hesitations, repetitions, interjections, memory lapses, etc. Language theories which focus upon linguistic competence would disregard such extraneous aspects of an individual's speaking performance.

Evaluation

Developmental theories are evaluated by their ability to predict correctly, logically, and parsimoniously. Each of the three language development theories is presently able to meet these criteria to a different degree.

The imitation-reinforcement theory of language development is parsimonious and predicts some aspects of language development, such as the *sequence* of language acquisition, logically and correctly. However, it is unable to explain or predict other language phenomena. For example, children do not hear words like *comed*, *doed*, and *breaked* in their environment. Yet children use such words in their speech and, despite a lack of reinforcement for the use of such words, children persist in using them for relatively long periods of time. Likewise, expressions like "All gone sticky" and "Billy down" are formulated by children even though they could not have heard such expressions.

The imitation-reinforcement theory of language development also does not adequately explain how children discover which portions of their speech are grammatically incorrect. Since the parents typically reinforce the truth value of a statement rather than the grammatical correctness of a statement, children are often reinforced for grammatically incorrect statements, and not reinforced for grammatically correct statements. For example, when children say "Mama isn't a boy, he a girl" (Brown and Hanlon 1970) his parents are likely to say "That's right." Yet, when the child points to a lighthouse and says "There's the animal farm" (Brown, Cazden, and Bellugi 1969) his parents are likely to say "No, that's a lighthouse."

Finally, the imitation-reinforcement theory of language development cannot account for the early and rapid acquisition of language. Also, research does not substantiate some imitation-reinforcement explanations of language acquisition. For example, imitation-reinforcement theorists propose that children learn language by imitating their parents' sentence expansions. Cazden (1965) used this language training approach with young children and reported little improvement in the children's language performance. The imitation-reinforcement theory of language development, then, fits the criterion of parsimony, but does not predict correctly or logically many known language phenomena. Therefore, developmental psychologists have a tendency to view this theory of language development as inadequate.

The nativist theory is also subject to criticism according to the evaluation criteria of developmentalists. Nativists postulate both innate knowledge of language universals and innate processing mechanisms. These inborn abilities can account for the early acquisition of language, the existence of linguistic mistakes such as overgeneralizations, and the ability of individuals to comprehend and produce sentences which they have never heard or used before. The nativistic theory therefore predicts correctly and logically known linguistic phenomena. However, the rule-learning theory of language development also is able to correctly predict and logically explain these phenomena in a more parsimonious way because it postulates fewer innate abilities.

Innate abilities cannot be directly verified and should be taken as adequate explanations only when other explanations that are more parsimonious are disproven. Rule-learning theory, which postulates fewer innate mechanisms, accounts for the same linguistic phenomena as nativist theory. It must then be disproven by nativists in order for the nativist theory to meet the judgmental criteria for theory development. Therefore, the rule-learning theory of language development most adequately meets the evaluation criteria for an acceptable theory at the present time. However, present knowledge and research in the area of language development is limited. Other explanations have not yet been postulated or tested. For example, children may learn how to process language during the months prior to speech; that is, they may learn how to learn language. A theory such as this would explain linguistic phenomena in a correct, logical, and parsimonious manner without having to assume any innate processing abilities. This theory is a hypothetical possibility which remains to be proven or disproven, and it emphasizes that much is left to be learned in this area of language development.

SEMANTIC DEVELOPMENT

The process of language development involves more than learning how to combine phonemes, morphemes, and words into the patterns designated by a specific language. The child must also learn the meaning of the sound patterns of a language. Producing a sound pattern like "car go" in order to communicate that a cookie is wanted would not be understood, and the desire for a cookie would be unfulfilled. The child must acquire word meanings as well as sound patterns to communicate successfully. The area of language development concerned with the acquisition of meaning is semantics.

The construction of semantic development theories has been hampered by knowledge deficits which do not affect the construction of theories of sound patterns and syntax. Syntactic theorists are able to use grammar as a means of categorizing, analyzing, and comparing syntactic data. Semantic theorists do not have such a tool for utilizing semantic data. Syntactic theorists have been able to identify the components of adult syntactic competence. Semantic theorists are uncertain of the components of adult semantic competence; their framework for the collection and analysis of data from children's speech and their criteria for comparing adult semantic competence and the semantic development of children is questionable. The development of syntax and sound patterns can be separated from other areas of the child's development; the development of linguistic meaning is difficult to separate from cognitive development. As Dale (1972) points out, it is difficult to neatly separate the semantic question "How do children express ideas?" from the cognitive question "What kind of ideas do children have to express?" These difficulties and others inherent in the construction of developmental theories make semantic development one of the least understood areas of human development.

Children's acquisition of meaning can be described in three stages. During the first stage children use single words to convey the meaning of an entire sentence. During the second stage, they combine words into sentences but the meaning of the words and word combinations often is not completely understood by the children. In the final stage, children have acquired semantic competence; they use words, phrases, and sentences meaningfully.

The child's first single-word utterances commonly consist of duplicated monosyllables such as *mama* and *dada*, called holophrases. Holophrases refer to total happenings not precisely defined as things or actions and they convey a variety of meanings. For example, *mama* may mean "Here is mama," "Where is mama?" "Come here, mama," or "I need mama." The meaning of the word *mama* is contingent upon the situation or circumstances in which it is said. As the child's repertoire of words increases, more words are used in this manner. At this stage, the child's speech consists of a vocabulary of single words; each word corresponds to, and carries the meaning of

In the final stage in the acquisition of meaning, the child uses words, phrases, and sentences correctly.

a variety of sentences. Theorists describe a child at the first stage as speaking with a sentence dictionary; each word corresponds to, or is paired with, a variety of sentence meanings.

As a child's vocabulary enlarges, communication through holophrases becomes inefficient, cumbersome, and susceptible to ambiguity (Hopper and Naremore 1973). At this time, the child begins to formulate sentences and constructs a word dictionary. A word dictionary contains the words in a child's vocabulary together with the meanings the child attributes to these words. While individual words have meaning, they gain additional meaning when they are combined into sentences. The use of a word dictionary to construct sentences marks the beginning of the second stage in the acquisition of meaning. It coincides with the emergence of syntax in the child's speech and is somewhat dependent upon syntax. The child must know how to order or sequence words correctly according to the grammatical structure of the language before the child can construct meaningful sentences. For example, the sentences "A dog bit Billy" and "Billy bit a dog" contain the same words and word meanings, but convey different sentence meanings because of different syntactic structure.

Although a young child's word dictionary during this stage is similar to that of an adult, it is not as extensive. As McNeill (1970) points out, the individual words in an adult's dictionary are semantically "fuller" and more precise than those of a young child, probably because entries in the child's dictionary are incomplete. Not all of the semantic features associated with a word enter the dictionary when the word itself enters. For example, a child might know that *ball* refers to a round object of various sizes and colors and may know what to do with one. But the child may not know that *ball* means something entirely different in the sentence, "Cinderella went to the ball." It seems that the acquisition of a word dictionary is a sequential process. The child gradually learns the various properties associated with a word after the word has entered the child's "dictionary." Thus semantic development during the second stage consists of the completion of the existent dictionary entries as well as the acquisition of new words.

Movement from stage two to stage three in the acquisition of meaning occurs at approximately eight years of age. (This movement seems to occur as an increased number of specific properties are added to a word's definition.) These properties are thought to be similar to syntactic rules (Katz and Fodor 1963) and are subdivided into two types: semantic features or markers, and selection restrictions.

A semantic feature or marker expresses a part of the meaning of a word; and several semantic features together add up to a word meaning. The semantic features of a word resemble the dictionary definition of that word. For example *dog* has among other semantic features *furry*, *barks*, and *four legs*. A specific semantic feature may be attached to more than one word. For example the semantic feature *living* is attached to *dogs*, *cats*, *people*, and *plants* as well as to many other words. The attachment of a specific semantic feature to a group of words suggests that the meanings of the words have something in common. Generally, the more mutual semantic markers words possess, the closer the words are in meaning.

Selection restrictions are rules that specify the positions in which a word may be used with consistent meaning. When selection restrictions are violated, nonsensical or anomalous sentences such as "The door eats the cereal" result. The semantic features of the word *door* do not match the selection restrictions of the word *eats* since *eats* can describe only animate nouns and the semantic features of *door* do not include *animate*. Matching semantic features with selection restrictions often causes problems for children when they begin to combine words. If children's concept of a given word does not contain all of the necessary semantic features, then errors will occur when the child begins to combine the word with other words. If a dictionary entry lacks certain crucial semantic features, it will also lack the selection restrictions that are based upon them. Young children will accept grammatical combinations of words that an adult or older child with a complete semantic dictionary would mark as anomalous. For example, children who do not know that *inanimate* is a semantic feature of *a cold* might say "A cold caught me"; they do not have the selection restriction which specifies that the verb referring to *a cold* must be inactive because *a cold* is inanimate.

It is believed that the acquisition of semantic features and selection restrictions occurs simultaneously with the acquisition of concepts. Words are symbols of concepts, and the properties of words correspond to the properties of the concepts they represent. The semantic feature *living* applies to the word *dog* just as the concept *living* applies to the word *dog*. Language theorists hypothesize that the acquisition of semantic features and selection restrictions are closely related. They postulate that the semantic properties of a word become more complete and accurate as the concept symbolized by the word is broadened.

IMPLICATIONS OF LANGUAGE DEVELOPMENT THEORIES FOR IGE

By the time children begin school, most have achieved a great deal of linguistic competence. They have discovered the phonemes of their language and they have determined, through inductive, deductive, or imitative processes, all of the basic sentence patterns and rules governing their language. Most five- and six-year-olds also exhibit extensive receptive, comprehension vocabularies. The average five-year-old has a "word dictionary" which contains anywhere from 2700 to 3000 entries. The average kindergartener has learned many of the basic language concepts and understands the meaning of words which symbolize fundamental qualities (words like *big, short*), quantities (words such as *few, some, more*), spatial relations (words such as *far, under, top*) and temporal relationships (words such as *before, after, soon*). The linguistic performance levels of beginning school children are also impressive. The speech of most kindergarteners is 100 percent intelligible. Their expressive vocabularies, words which they can use meaningfully in spontaneous speech, are well developed although they are not as large as their receptive vocabularies. Children as well as adults understand more words than they themselves use.

The "typical kindergartner" and the "average five-year-old" are no more homogeneous in language development than they are in other areas of development; they exhibit many interindividual differences. Some kindergarteners possess linguistic skills which the majority of their peers will not demonstrate for several months or years. Others barely meet the minimal requirements for school attendance. The individual child, too, is likely to have progressed at different developmental rates in acquiring the sound patterns, the grammar, and the semantics of the language. A child may, for example, show perfect mastery of the phonemes of the language, but a poor understanding of its structure and semantics. Some children show a broad discrepancy between their linguistic competence and their linguistic performance.

It has been found that approximately 5 percent of school-age children exhibit deviant language behavior, and of these, over three-quarters have articulation defects (Telford and Sawrey 1967). "Articulation defects" refer to deviant sound patterning or the deviant production and arrangement of phonemes and morphemes into units of speech. Most children, when they begin school, have mastered almost all of the phonemes of Standard American English. The more difficult phonemes to produce, however, may not be completely acquired by many children. It is very common for five- and six-year-olds to make errors in producing the *t* sound, the *v*, the *s*, the *sh*, and *ch* sounds, the *j* sound (as in juice), the *r* and both of the *th* sounds. Children who cannot make these sounds correctly most often use other English phonemes as substitutes. They will substitute a *w* for the *r*, for example. Other children omit difficult sounds from words. Phoneme blends such as *bl*, *sp*, and *str* are difficult for many young children, so they often "drop" one of the sounds in the blend; they may say "sring" for "string," for example. Young children may also "distort" certain phonemes; they may articulate certain phonemes incorrectly, rather than replacing them with other sounds or omitting them entirely.

The responsibilities of the teacher in this area of language development is to recognize articulation errors. The teacher must also decide which articulation errors are within a normal range and which are truly deviant. Special attention to young children who exhibit minor or common phoneme misarticulations is unnecessary; they will most likely outgrow their errors. However, the 9-, 10-, or 11-year-old who has not mastered all of the sounds of American English may benefit from speech therapy, especially if the child is disturbed by the misarticulations. Kindergarteners and first and second graders whose speech is unintelligible or difficult to understand due to many errors in phoneme production may also need the help of a speech and language specialist. Teachers can foster the development of sound patterning abilities in children who show mild deviations from their peers. Phonics activities, which actually teach children to recognize the phonemes of their language and which encourage them to produce sounds correctly, can be helpful. Phonics games and activities can be especially useful to the student who is having difficulty mastering the alphabet or learning to read and spell because of poorly developed sound patterning abilities.

Syntactic Development

Nativists, rule-learning theorists, and imitation-reinforcement theorists all agree that one's linguistic environment is a critical ingredient in the acquisition of syntax. They disagree as to how syntactic rules are acquired and each credits the human organism with a different role in the process. But they do not disagree that children learn the structural rules governing language from the language they hear. This implies that most individual differences in syntactic development among school children can be attributed to different linguistic environments. Some parents are very verbal; they talk to their children frequently and extensively. Other children may have had limited opportunities to hear and use language, either inside or outside the home. The quality of children's linguistic environments varies also. Some children hear a great deal of language, but it may be language which lacks syntactic complexity and diversity. Some children grow up in bilingual or bidialectical linguistic environments. Others have grown up in homes and neighborhoods where Standard American English is not the preferred language. All of these variations in linguistic environment will create differences in syntactic development among school children.

The linguistic environment of the school can make a significant contribution to the development of syntactic competence in students. Although most children begin school having acquired all of the basic structures of their language, the development of syntax continues for a long time. The school is in the position to establish an environment where syntax is used correctly and effectively. Students can profit from hearing their language spoken correctly, according to the rules

Phonics games can be useful to students having certain language difficulties.

Students' linguistic environments differ.

of Standard American English. Good syntactic models can be especially valuable to children who have heard only a minimum of grammatically correct spoken language. Linguists have begun to discover that children pick up much of their linguistic knowledge from speaking and listening to their peers rather than to adult models. Teachers can put this to the advantage of students by encouraging the effective use of syntax among students. For example, in Bear Creek Elementary School, a school using IGE methods in Jefferson County, Colorado, Mrs. Vivian employed a language arts unit called "Just Me" to teach Karla and some of her peers the appropriate use of first person pronouns and adjectives. This unit began with incomplete sentences such as "I am _____" to which adjectives were to be added. Gradually, Karla and her peers were required to furnish more of the words for the sentences, then complete sentences, and successfully completed the unit when they were able to tell a story about themselves to the group using correct sentence structure.

Almost all school environments also provide formal instruction in the syntax or grammar of the standard language. This has traditionally been accepted as an effective means of promoting syntactic competence. IGE teachers have available a wealth of curriculum materials for teaching grammar to individual students, or to groups of students whose syntactic competence is poorly developed. A language arts curriculum which includes grammar can also help students to transfer their syntactic competence to linguistic performance; it encourages them to use syntax in oral and written communication.

In selecting and implementing syntactic development programs, IGE teachers should be aware of the theoretical differences among various curriculum materials. Transformational grammar is based upon the nativist theory of language development. Older methods of teaching syntax are oriented toward rule-learning and imitation-reinforcement theories. Proponents of each approach often contend that theirs is the most effective approach. Because of a lack of conclusive research, no single method can be advocated for all students. It is possible, however, that one method will prove more effective for an individual student. Teachers in IGE schools can determine whether one or the other or a combination of methods is most appropriate for each student, and provide the student with the best means to learn syntax by following instructional programming for the individual student.

Semantic Development

Semantics, or the acquisition of meaning, is an area of language development in which individual differences are perhaps most important with respect to successful learning. A student must perceive the meaning of what is said or written in order to understand it. Unfortunately, semantic development is also probably the area of language development which is least understood. Thus the best means of nurturing semantic development can only be hypothesized.

Since the acquisition of meaning and the acquisition of concepts are closely related, semantic competence may be fostered through methods similar to those used for facilitating concept formation. A possible method for facilitating the acquisition of meaning follows:

1. Provide clear instances when a word is used correctly and/or incorrectly.

2. Define the word, delineating its semantic features and synonymous words.

3. Indicate the nature of the word to be learned (i.e., a word referring to concrete objects, a word used as a descriptor, a word signifying an abstract idea).

4. Provide for proper sequencing of words to be learned, and of properties of words to be learned.

5. Encourage the students to discover instances where the word is used or could be used.

6. Provide situations in which the word could be used.

7. Encourage evaluation of word usage.

This method can be used to teach new words and words which are partially acquired, but not semantically "full." It can be employed in group settings, or in one-to-one situations.

An example of this method applied in a group setting at the second grade level for the word *coach* is:

1. The teacher provides correct instances in which the word *coach* is used, such as "The coach was drawn by horses," "The coach car on the train was full of people," "The coach taught the team to play baseball," and "Coach the team."

2. The teacher presents the semantic features of coach with reference to specific usage (i.e., A coach is a four-wheeled object drawn by horses which carries people; A coach is a section in a train, bus, or airplane which carries people; A coach is a person who helps other people to learn a skill; To coach means to help another person learn). The teacher may also present synonyms for the specific usages of the word 'coach' (i.e., a carriage, a cart, a teacher, a director, helping, teaching).

3. The teacher states that *coach* is both a word referring to a concrete object, a particular kind of person, and a descriptive word. The teacher explains that coach may be an object which carries people, a person who helps others to learn, or the act of helping another to learn.

4. The teacher explains the meaning of *coach* as an object and as a person before trying to explain the act of coaching but does not try to teach the meaning of the word *coach* to students before they know the semantic properties of the words *horse* (i.e., an animal that is able to pull objects such as plows and carts), *train* (a machine that has cars for carrying objects and people) and *learn* (to find out about something).

5. The teacher may ask questions like "Who coaches the school baseball team?" or show pictures of coaches or coaching, or ask students to find sentences in which the word *coach* is or can be used.

6. The teacher may ask students to read books such as *Cinderella*, in which the word *coach* is used, or talk about sports.

7. The teacher may ask if *coach* can be used in sentences like "The coach talked to his team," "The coach started itself," "The coach was behind the engine of the train," and "The coach car always carries coal."

An example of how semantic development was incorporated into the language arts curriculum at Bear Creek Elementary School is the unit entitled "Let's Pretend." In this unit new nouns are introduced such as *kangaroo*, and the students are required to perform a charade, acting out an incomplete sentence in which one of the semantic markers of the word is missing such as "If I were a kangaroo, I would _____ (hop)." Classmates are required to fill in the missing semantic feature in the sentence.

The example above is one of many examples which can be used to foster semantic development in the classroom. Other concept formation methods are available and, with modification, can be used. However, few curriculum materials or programs actually designed to further semantic development exist. Rather, vocabulary-building programs, which omit some of the important steps necessary for semantic development, have been designed and are available. Vocabulary-building programs can be used as a basis for a semantic development program, but teachers must be aware of the omitted steps in such programs and supplement them accordingly.

SUGGESTED READINGS FOR CHAPTER 4

DiVesta, F. J. 1974. *Language, learning, and cognitive processes.* Monterey, Calif.: Brooks/Cole.

The concept of language is defined and the reader is offered insight into the ways in which the elements of language (e.g., phonemes, morphemes, and so forth) relate to the processes of learning, recall, and transfer of information. Qualitative differences in cognitive functioning and language acquisition are described at distinctive development stages and within various experiential settings.

Brown, R. W., and C. Hanlon 1970. Derivational complexity and order of acquisition in child speech. In J. R. Hayes (ed.), *Cognition and the development of language.* New York: Wiley.

Stemming from their belief that a more comprehensive understanding of the developmental sequence in the acquisition of meaning is necessary, the authors present an experimental program designed to explore the psychological correlates of such grammatical structures as transformations and phrase markers. Serving as the theoretical basis of the program is their contention that a step-by-step correspondence exists between the sequence of grammatical rules necessary to process a sentence and the sequence of psychological functions utilized as a person processes the sentence.

Chomsky, N. 1968. *Language and mind.* New York: Harcourt.

In his critique of past and contemporary contributions to the ongoing research on the nature of language development, Chomsky places special emphasis on the role of innate factors in language development. From his nativist position, Chomsky supports his view that language learners have an innate mechanism which allows them to construct, test, and evaluate hypotheses concerning the structure of a particular language by citing examples and sociological research.

REFERENCES

Bellugi-Klima, U. 1968. Linguistic mechanisms underlying child speech. In E. M. Zale (ed.), *Proceedings of the conference on language and language behavior.* New York: Appleton-Century-Crofts.

Berko, J. 1958. The child's learning of English morphology. *Word.* 14: 150–177.

Braine, M. D. S. 1965. On the bias of phrase structure: a reply to Bever, Fodor and Weksel. *Psychological Review* 72: 483–492   .

Brown, R. W. 1965. *Social psychology.* New York: Free Press.

———, and U. Bellugi 1964. Three processes in the child's acquisition of syntax. *Harvard Educational Review* 34:133–151.

———, C. Cazden, and U. Bellugi 1969. The child's grammar from one to three. In J. Hill (ed.), *1967 Minnesota symposia on child psychology.* Vol. 2. Minneapolis: University of Minnesota Press.

———, and C. Fraser, 1964. The acquisition of syntax. In U. Bellugi and R. Brown (eds.), *The acquisition of language.* Monograph of the Society for Research in Child Development 29, (Seria No. 92).

———, and C. Hanlon 1970. Derivational complexity and order of acquisition in child speech. In J. R. Hayes (ed.), *Cognition and the development of language.* New York: Wiley.

Cazden, C. 1965. Environmental assistance to the child's acquisition of grammar. Unpublished doctoral dissertation. Harvard University Graduate School of Education.

Chomsky, N. 1968. *Language and mind.* New York: Harcourt.

——— 1965. *Aspects of the theory of syntax.* Cambridge: M.I.T. Press.

Dale, P. S. 1972. *Language development structure and function.* Hinsdale, Ill.: Dryden.

Ervin, S. M. 1964. Imitation and structural change in children's language. In E. H. Lenneberg (ed.) *New directions in the study of language*. Cambridge: M.I.T. Press.

Gibran, K. 1923. *The prophet*. New York: Knopf.

Hockett, C. F. 1960. The origin of speech. *Scientific American* 203(3): 89–96.

Hopper, R., and R. Naremore 1973. *Children's speech*. New York: Harper & Row.

Katz, J. J. 1966. *The philosophy of language*. New York: Harper & Row.

———, and J. A. Fodor 1963. The structure of a semantic theory. *Language* 39: 170–210.

Lenneberg, E. H. 1962. Understanding language without ability to speak. *Journal of Abnormal and Social Psychology* 65: 419–425.

——— 1964. A biological perspective of language. In E. H. Lenneberg (ed.), *New directions in the study of language*. Cambridge: M.I.T. Press.

McNeill, D. 1970. *The acquisition of language: the study of developmental psycholinguistics*. New York: Harper & Row.

——— 1966. Developmental psycholinguistics. In F. L. Smith and G. A. Miller (eds.), *The genesis of language*. Cambridge: M.I.T. Press.

Mowrer, O. H. 1960. *Learning theory and the symbolic process*. New York: Wiley.

Skinner, B. F. 1957. *Verbal behavior*. New York: Appleton-Century-Crofts.

Slobin, D. I. 1966. Comments on "Developmental Psycholinguistics." In F. L. Smith and G. A. Miller (eds.), *The genesis of language*. Cambridge: M.I.T. Press.

Staats, A. W. 1968. *Learning, language, and cognition*. New York: Holt.

——— 1961. Verbal habit-families, concepts, and the operant conditioning of word classes. *Psychological Review* 68: 190–204.

Telford, C., and J. Sawrey 1967. *The exceptional individual: psychological and educational aspects*. Englewood Cliffs, N.J.: Prentice-Hall.

5

Affective Development

Objectives

Upon completion of this chapter, the reader should be able:

■ To recognize the interrelationship among intrapsychic factors, need factors, and social-psychological factors in affective development.

■ To understand Erikson's theory of affective-psychosocial development.

■ To comprehend Maslow's needs theory and how it influences affective development.

■ To understand Bandura and Walters's social learning theory.

■ To compare the theories of Erikson, Maslow, and Bandura and Walters.

■ To articulate ways that affective development may be nurtured through IGE.

If a child lives with criticism,
He learns to condemn.
If a child lives with hostility,
He learns to fight.
If a child lives with ridicule,
He learns to be shy.
If a child lives with shame,
He learns to feel guilty.
If a child lives with encouragement,
He learns confidence.
If a child lives with praise,
He learns to appreciate.
If a child lives with fairness,
He learns justice.
If a child lives with security,
He learns to have faith.
If a child lives with approval,
He learns to like himself.
If a child lives with acceptance and friendship,
He learns to find love in the world.

Dorothy Law Holte

THEORIES OF AFFECTIVE DEVELOPMENT

It was John's first day of school, and he was filled with apprehension. He felt safe in his mother's presence but knew she intended to leave him at school and return home. Her promise to be waiting for him at lunchtime gave him little comfort, for lunchtime seemed an eternity away. The other children going into Unit A with their mothers also gave little comfort to John. His family had recently moved to this neighborhood, and the other children present were strangers. So were the unit teachers who greeted children and mothers as they arrived. John's grasp on his mother's hand grew tighter as they arrived at the classroom door. One of the unit teachers, Miss Jane, detected John's apprehension, and suggested that John's mother stay for awhile. Relief!

Still grasping his mother's hand John now began to notice things around him. The big blocks in the corner looked interesting. The piano was familiar and reassuring, for it reminded John of past good times when his mother had played for him. John's grasp on his mother's hand weakened. John was on his way to a pleasant school experience.

John's initial reaction to his first day of school can be described by three interrelated factors: (1) need states, (2) intrapsychic states, and (3) social-psychological circumstances. A need state is a natural want toward which an individual strives. John's dominant want was safety. An intrapsychic state is an internal emotional feeling. John's intrapsychic state was apprehension. A social-psychological circumstance is an external situation which alters one's need state and intrapsychic state. John's social-psychological circumstance of being in a strange place filled with unknown people increased his need for safety and his feeling of apprehension. Later, the social-psychological circumstance of his mother staying with him fulfilled his need for safety and decreased his apprehension.

John's initial emotional response to his first day of school is not unusual. Most individuals feel some degree of apprehension when they enter an unfamiliar situation. It is considered a normal human response. However, individuals do differ with respect to the types of situations which induce apprehension, the amount of apprehension a particular situation induces, and the manner in which they handle their apprehensive feelings. The similarities as well as the differences in emotional responses among individuals can be accounted for by the same three factors which described John's emotional response. Need states, intrapsychic states, and social-psychological circumstances describe emotional responses because they are the factors which produce emotional responses.

One of John's teachers was able to decrease his apprehension because she recognized and altered one of the factors which was producing John's apprehension, his need for safety, and his fear of "losing" the safety of his mother. Other emotional situations which occur both in and out of school can be handled similarly. Whenever one of the factors which is producing an emotional response changes or is changed, the nature of the emotional response itself changes. The person who is able to recognize and consciously alter the factors producing emotional responses is able to control emotional situations. Such an individual possesses the capability of helping or hindering the affective development of others through the individual's actions.

Most individuals either consciously or unconsciously have some awareness of the factors underlying emotional responses. Emotional responses do not continue indefinitely. Either consciously or unconsciously people are able to alter the emotional situations and responses of themselves and others through changing the underlying factors. However, only those individuals who are consciously aware of each factor underlying an emotional response, the strength of each factor, the interplay among factors, and how to alter one or another factor, can consciously control emotional situations and teach others how to do so. Only such individuals can successfully promote affective development in others and, at the same time, avoid inadvertently hindering it.

Individuals who have achieved some degree of self-understanding are more likely to be consciously aware of the factors underlying emotional responses. They have studied these factors both in themselves and others in the process of learning about themselves. Consequently, such individuals are more likely to be able to promote affective development because of their conscious awareness and ability to control the factors underlying affective development. Teachers should be able to consciously control the affective situations in their classrooms, consciously decide what is best for the affective development of their students, and consciously foster in their students the abilities necessary for handling such situations themselves. This chapter provides information which can aid teachers in achieving conscious awareness and control of both their own emotional situations and the affective development of others.

Erikson's Psychosocial Theory

Erik Erikson (1950) focuses on the intrapsychic factor of affective development. He proposes that internal emotional feelings develop in a sequence of eight stages, each stage corresponding to a certain period of time in an individual's life. At each stage, according to Erikson, individuals develop either a positive or negative feeling about themselves through internalizing the attitudes of others toward their behavior. Erikson's theory is termed a psychosocial theory because of the initial strong influence of social circumstances on the development of internal emotional feelings. Erikson admits that later in life individuals can alter their initial internal feelings about themselves by being presented with strong contradictory social attitudes. However, he suggests that the influence of social circumstances at the time in which the initial feeling developed, together with the already established internal feeling, make a change of emotions more difficult once the significant developmental stage is past.

Erikson views the positive resolution of his stages by adults who are in contact with children as influential in the child's resolution of the stages. He believes that if teachers have positively resolved their prior affective stages, then their students will be more likely to resolve the stage they are at positively, and perhaps even change negative decisions made in prior stages. Through the cycle of successive generations, the potential affective development of people can be furthered by teachers who have resolved Erikson's stages in a positive fashion.

Trust versus Mistrust

Erikson's first stage is the stage of trust versus mistrust. This stage begins at birth and is resolved positively or negatively by approximately the age of one or one and a half. It is during this period that infants develop a basic trust or mistrust of others through their relationship with their parents. If infants find that their parents respond to their needs, they develop trust. They become less reluctant to let their parents out of their fields of vision, because they trust that the parents will return if they need them. Erikson emphasizes that the amount of trust which infants develop will depend upon the quality of the parent-child relationship. If adequate trust does not develop during this stage, children will develop a distrust of other people, which may lead to unhappiness and considerable personality difficulties later in life.

Autonomy versus Doubt

The second psychosocial stage is that of autonomy versus shame and doubt. This stage begins at approximately age one or one and a half, and is resolved by approximately age three. During this period children try to establish some degree of independence by doing things themselves. If they are allowed to do tasks of which they are capable and which they want to do, they develop confidence in their abilities. If, on the other hand, parents consistently do the children's tasks for them or criticize their efforts, young children develop doubt in their abilities and shame in the results of their efforts.

Initiative versus Guilt

Erikson's third psychosocial stage is called the stage of initiative versus guilt. This stage begins at approximately age three and is resolved by approximately age five or six. Children at this stage no longer rely on others to provide tasks for them. They decide what they wish to do, begin to do it themselves, and ask for help when they need it. If their parents respond with encouragement and praise, children develop a positive feeling about initiating tasks. If their parents respond by discouraging children's initiative, criticizing it, or ignoring the children when they ask for help, they develop a sense of guilt about performing tasks which they had not been specifically told to do. This guilt, if it remains, can cause individuals to become considerably overcontrolled and excessively inhibited.

Industry versus Inferiority

The next stage is known as the stage of industry versus inferiority. This stage begins at about the age of six or seven and lasts until the onset of puberty. During this stage children enjoy projects and activities involving concrete objects. They will spend large amounts of time in adultlike occupations, collecting, making, and studying objects. If children receive approval and assurance from others that their projects and activities are worthwhile endeavors, and are praised and rewarded upon completion of their endeavors, they develop a sense of self-worth and positive feelings about becoming involved in activities. If children's projects and activities are viewed by others as "making a mess," silly, and worthless, or if their finished projects are degraded, children develop a sense of inferiority and negative feelings about becoming involved in other activities.

The student at Erikson's fourth stage enjoys collecting things.

Identity versus Role Confusion

Erikson's fifth psychosocial stage, that of identity versus role confusion, covers the period from puberty to young adulthood. During this stage, adolescents seek to establish a realistic perception of themselves by integrating all they know about themselves. The feedback individuals receive from their peers becomes extremely important at this time. If peers clarify and refine individuals' perception of themselves, and accept them as they are, individuals achieve a realistic and satisfactory self-identity. If peers distort and muddy individuals' perceptions of themselves, and reject them unless they conform to the peers' perceptions, individuals become confused and are unable to discover realistic and satisfactory self-identities.

Intimacy versus Isolation

Erikson's sixth psychosocial stage, intimacy versus isolation, extends from young adulthood until early middle age. During young adulthood, individuals seek stable interpersonal relationships either through marriage or friendship. If individuals are able to share with others, care about others, and are not afraid of being engulfed by the desires of others, and if others respond similarly, the individuals achieve the benefits of intimate relationships. If individuals are unable to care or share or are afraid of becoming too close to others, or if the others in their life are unable to establish intimate relationships, individuals become isolated from close human contact: persons alone in an uncaring world.

Generativity versus Self-absorption

Generativity versus self-absorption is the seventh stage of Erikson's hierarchy and corresponds with the period of life termed middle age. At this time individuals organize their perception of the world and establish their societal role. If they view the world as a worthwhile place in which to live, they interact with it and actively work to make it better for succeeding generations. If they view the world as an ugly place in which to live, they criticize it and withdraw from it, becoming engulfed by personal needs.

Integrity versus Despair

The last stage in Erikson's sequence, integrity versus despair, corresponds with old age. During this stage individuals reflect upon their life's accomplishments. If they perceive their past with satisfaction, they feel contentment. If they perceive their past as a series of mistakes, they feel despair for they cannot live life over again.

Maslow's Needs Theory

Abraham H. Maslow (1943, 1968a, 1968b, 1970) focuses on the need factor of affective development. He believes humans have certain inborn needs which they strive to fulfill. These inborn needs form a hierarchy in which the satisfaction of lower level needs take precedence over the satisfaction of higher level needs. Individuals who are seeking to fulfill needs perceive and react to situations in ways colored by their needs.

Maslow describes human needs in biological terms. He believes every need arises from an imbalance or disequilibrium between what humankind's nature deems necessary for the health of a person, and what a person's environment provides. When the environment provides people with what they need, homeostasis or equilibrium occurs. When individuals' environments do not provide them with what they need, they remain in a state of disequilibrium and continue to strive for that which their nature deems necessary. If a person remains in a state of disequilibrium for a long period of time that person becomes ill either physically, mentally, or both and may no longer be able to obtain from the environment what is necessary for a return to health. Environmental factors thus strongly influence a person's physical and mental condition because they regulate need fulfillment.

Humankind's nature is the precipitating force in Maslow's needs theory. It decides what is healthy for humans, and motivates people toward what is good for them both personally and as members of society. Maslow views each individual as having a slightly different nature from other individuals. The unfolding of a person's nature through proper environmental stimulation and nurturance creates unique individuals who make healthy contributions to society. Maslow describes a person whose inner nature is in the process of unfolding as "becoming that which he is capable of being."

Maslow's interest in human needs leads him to formulate a theoretical hierarchy which reflects the sequence in which he postulates needs must be fulfilled. Figure 5.1 depicts his hierarchy. This hierarchy can be divided into two parts. The first part is composed of basic needs which must be met in the process of individuals becoming that which they are capable of being. The second part is composed of meta-needs which are the needs of individuals whose basic needs have been fulfilled, and who have become that which their inner nature directed them to be.

Physiological Needs

The first level in Maslow's hierarchy consists of physiological needs such as the need for food and shelter. These needs are the outgrowth of the will to survive. Maslow views them as arising from the nature

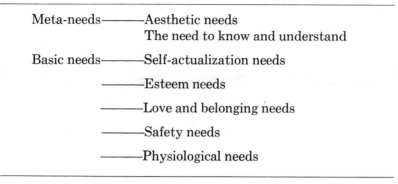

Fig. 5.1 Maslow's hierarchy of needs.

of humans as living, physical organisms. Physiological homeostasis in which body temperature, blood pressure, etc. are at their normal level is the desired, healthy state of being. Physiological disequilibrium is the undesired, unhealthy state of being in which physical needs are unfulfilled. Physiological disequilibrium is inferred from an individual's behavior. When a person is hungry and trying to find something to eat, the body "needs" food for energy. When a person is thirsty and looking for something to drink, the person "needs" liquid. The need for physiological homeostasis begins at conception. While a baby is within the womb, nutrients are automatically supplied through the mother's body. After leaving the self-sufficient environment of the womb, a child makes needs known initially by crying and later through the use of language. The child is still reliant on the environment to fulfill needs.

If the physiological needs of individuals are not met, all other needs become irrelevant. Satisfying physiological needs becomes the primary purpose of their behavior. If physiological needs are great enough, individuals will even disregard their own safety in order to meet them. The importance of physiological equilibrium in school children should not be underestimated. Disadvantaged children who come to school hungry every day are not going to learn or achieve. Their attention is focused on satisfying their need for food. Their growling, churning stomachs prevent them from attending to multiplication tables, spelling lists, and other learning tasks. Their need for food must be met and physiological homeostasis achieved before they can focus attention upon activities not related to obtaining food. The federal government acknowledged the importance of satisfying physiological needs when it subsidized the school lunch program. However, many school children spend the hours between the start of the school day and lunchtime focused upon their physiological needs.

Safety Needs

The second level of needs in the hierarchy are safety needs. Safety needs consist of intrapsychic needs for psychological well-being as well as physical safety in the environment. Infants have special needs for psychological safety when they are physically ill, or experience bad dreams, disturbed schedules, or a breakup of their family. Examples such as these are at a very basic level. As children mature, safety needs tend to become broadened. As persons grow older, they need to have some control over their environment. Things like job security and an assured retirement income may also be viewed as meeting safety needs in addition to those acts which meet temporal physical safety needs. Thus, safety needs imply a need for a world which is orderly and manageable for the individual, an environment which affords homeostasis in terms of the individual's need to be safe.

In most circumstances in the United States, physiological and safety needs do not serve as important motivators because society gives some assurance that these needs will be met. In fact needs at this level may have been primary motivators for the creation of the society into which we have been born. Such regulatory systems meet the needs of individuals or they would cease to exist. The alternative to societal regulation would be anarchy in which each individual would be challenging others' rights to physiological satisfaction and safety.

Love and Belonging Needs

Just as the attainment of physiological security allowed safety needs to emerge, the attainment of physical and psychological safety allows higher order needs to become of primary importance. Next in the order of Maslow's hierarchy are love and belonging needs. These needs should not be confused with a need for sex which is largely a physiological need. Love and belonging needs concern affectionate relationships with others and the elimination of feelings of loneliness and alienation. These needs are met by feeling that one is a member of "the team" whether the team consists of a family unit, a congenial job relationship, or membership in a fraternal order.

Our industrial society seems to have disrupted our development at this level. When countries were largely agricultural in nature, family relationships and community relationships helped meet love and belonging needs because working together satisfied the human need for social contact. The establishment of the industrial complex

Maslow's love and belonging need level.

with its assembly lines, time clocks, and rapid mobility eliminated much of this satisfaction. As a result several generations have existed without the degree of warm and intimate contact with others that was experienced by their forefathers. Is this part of the reason for the youth rebellion against parental values? Are these unfulfilled needs the reason for the increasing maladjustment and even pathology evident in our society?

Esteem Needs

Maslow placed esteem needs at the fourth level of his hierarchy because most individuals need fulfillment of their love and belonging needs before esteem becomes a primary concern. However, in some individuals esteem takes precedence over love and belonging. In these individuals, a lack of fulfillment of esteem needs interferes with their ability to relate to others and maintain warm, affectionate relationships. The substantial number of individuals in which esteem needs precede love and belonging needs leads Maslow to theorize that the positions of love and belonging needs and esteem needs in his hierarchy are reversed for some individuals.

Esteem needs arise from the desire to feel that one is an adequate, competent, and capable person. Esteem needs are met when individuals are successful in their endeavors and when their success is acknowledged by others. For some individuals, status and prestige are the types of acknowledgment necessary for adequate self-esteem. For other individuals, confirmation of their success by others is sufficient for adequate self-esteem. In general, esteem needs are met through interacting with others who recognize one's competence.

Schools have a major responsibility for meeting needs at the esteem level. The lower level needs are more typically met through the responsibilities of the family. Families are the source of physiological need fulfillment. Safety needs are also met largely through the security offered in the home, as are love and belonging needs. When children embark upon school careers, however, their social interaction is largely in that setting. Therefore, schools have a responsibility to provide experiences in which students can be successful so that they may develop feelings of adequacy and competency. Such feelings of positive self-worth free individuals from preoccupation with esteem needs and they then can attend to their need to self-actualize.

Self-actualization Needs

The fifth level of Maslow's hierarchy consists of self-actualization needs, the last of Maslow's basic needs. According to Maslow, what

The school should meet the students' needs for self-esteem.

persons can become they must become in order to be happy and mentally healthy. Self-actualization is the process of becoming all one is capable of being. When the primary focus of individuals' attention is upon gaining self-knowledge and self-understanding in order to become all that their unique natures directs them to be, they are in the process of self-actualizing. When individuals have become all that they are capable of being at a particular time in their lives, they are momentarily self-actualized. However, since what individuals are capable of being changes throughout their lives, self-actualization is a constant, ongoing process of growth which continues throughout everyone's lifetime.

Schools have a responsibility to help individuals self-actualize. This can be accomplished by nurturing in all individuals self-understanding and awareness of their own individuality and inner nature. Providing opportunities for individuals to become that which their inner nature dictates is equally important. In order to successfully promote self-actualization, teachers must be aware of and attentive to the moments of discontentment in their students, and provide opportunities which are consonant with the students' motivational perspectives.

Aesthetic Needs and the Need to Know and Understand

Aesthetic needs and the need to know and understand Maslow terms meta-needs. Meta-needs are similar to basic needs in that they arise from the inner nature of human beings and are manifested by all individuals who have had their lower-level needs, basic needs, fulfilled. Meta-needs differ from basic needs in that they are not as dependent as basic needs upon societal interaction for fulfillment.

The need to know and understand refers to persons' innate curiosity about their surroundings. Humans are attracted to the unknown, the mysterious, the unexplained, and desire to explore, organize, and explain the phenomena they experience. Aesthetic needs encompass a craving for beauty. Almost everyone manifests a preference for beauty, symmetry, and structure. Most people enjoy watching a deer gracefully bound into the forest and would become disconcerted if the deer hobbled slowly along the roadside, contradicting its nature.

Schools and teachers have a responsibility to provide the materials necessary for fulfillment of students' meta-needs. Curiosity should be encouraged. Students should be provided opportunities and means for exploring, organizing, and analyzing the phenomena they experience. The school environment should be aesthetically pleasing. Students who wish to add to the beauty of the school setting should be encouraged in their endeavors.

Bandura and Walters's Social Learning Theory

Bandura and Walters (1963) focus upon the social-psychological factor of affective development. They propose that previous and present conditioning and modeling determine both the internal and external affective reactions of an individual. Both conditioning and modeling are included in their theory, for Bandura and Walters believe that reinforcement alone does not explain the rapidity of affective and social development.

The stimulus-response conditioning process as postulated by Skinner (see Chapter 3) is a portion of this social learning theory. Bandura and Walters maintain that an individual learns how to perform social acts through operant conditioning. However, unlike Skinner, Bandura and Walters admit that internal intermediary factors may be present during the conditioning process and may influence how an individual performs a social act.

The other portion of Bandura and Walters's theory emphasizes modeling or imitation. Imitation involves learning through observing the types of reinforcement others receive for particular social acts. When to perform a particular act, where to perform it, with whom to perform it, and so forth, are learned through imitation according to Bandura and Walters.

The people whom an individual observes and imitates are termed models, hence the synonym of modeling for imitation learning. The models which influence people include three types: real, symbolic, and representational. Parents, peers, and teachers are real models. Young children gain primary attitudes toward everyday situations through observing and imitating such models. The symbolic model is presented to the child orally, in written form, or in the form of pictures. Some examples of symbolic models are characters in fables, parables, biographies, and art. It is generally felt that these exemplary models play an important role in the socialization of children, in acquainting them with social norms, values, and ideals. The representational model is one portrayed by audiovisual methods, e.g., television or movies. Representational models are often considered to be quite influential upon children in visually oriented societies.

Modeling, or imitation learning, depends on the children's observation of cause and effect in their environment, rather than on direct reinforcement of the children's actions. Bandura and Walters note three possible effects of models on the behavior of children. The first is to bring about an entirely novel response, and occurs when children have no previous experience with the observed social behavior. In such instances, children assimilate the entire behavior and its effects. The speed and intensity of assimilation depends upon the environmental rewards or punishments the 'proper' response receives. The second effect of models pertains to previously learned behavior which becomes either more inhibited or less inhibited than it was prior to the children observing the model. In cases where a model's behavior is punished, the effect is to inhibit the future performance of that behavior by children. Should a model's behavior be either nonpun-

The younger student will often model the behavior of older students.

ished or rewarded, children are inclined to overcome any inhibitions they might feel toward performing that particular act, even though they or another model previously may have been punished for it. The third effect of observing a model is to elicit a similar response already in the children's behavior repertoire, even though they have not yet had the chance to perform this response, or have "forgotten" it. For example, children who are taken to the park will want to do what they observe the other children in the park are doing.

In addition to positive and negative reinforcements to the model, characteristics of the model and characteristics of the observer also affect the imitation learning process. Models who possess status, competence, power, nurturance, or a combination of these qualities are more likely to be imitated than those who lack these qualities. Observers usually gauge the status or prestige of a model by its clothes and possessions. High-status models, those with clothes and possessions the observer admires, will probably be imitated, while models with low-status, those with clothes and possessions the observer finds undesirable, will probably be ignored. The observer judges competence by the visible achievements of the model. The famous basketball player who works in the slums will provide a highly imitated model for young children there. Power refers to the degree of influence a model is considered to have in the observer's environment, in other words, the extent the model controls the distribution of rewards and punishments in the observer's world. Nurturance is defined as noncontingent affection, affection with no strings attached. It may be seen in parents who do not withdraw affection and support from their children regardless of what the children do. In general, nurturant, powerful, competent, and/or high-status models are highly imitated whereas nonnurturant, powerless, incompetent, and/or low-status models are ineffective.

Characteristics of observers which affect their degree of susceptibility to a model include self-esteem, dependency, perceived similarity to the model, and level of sensory arousal. Self-esteem, according to social learning theorists, is the result of consistent positive reinforcement for behavior and tasks. Observers with high self-esteem will supposedly feel little need to attend to alternative modes of dealing with their environment. They are satisfied with the status quo. Observers with low self-esteem will tend to alter their behavior to match a model's. Dependency is measured by the amount of help-seeking or suggestibility children exhibit. Independent children will tackle tasks within their range of ability on their own or with a minimum of supervision. Conversely, dependent children are quick to imitate the behaviors of a model. In fact, dependent children will usually assimilate all behaviors which the model exhibits, the extraneous along with the useful. Consequently dependent children will not learn from a model as efficiently as independent children, who attend only to those actions of a model which are instrumental to completing a task. Perceived similarity to the model also positively influences modeling behavior. The similarity may be external or internal in nature. Students are more likely to emulate teachers who are similar to themselves in appearance or disposition. Finally, the arousal or stress level of children, that is, their level of sensory alertness, also affects their tendency to imitate the behavior of a model. Alert children are more likely to perceive the relevant aspects of a model's behavior and thus are able to copy the model's behavior with greater accuracy than children who are not alert.

Bandura and Walters developed their social learning theory of modeling from experiments they performed with children. These experiments focused upon the actions of children in contrived situations after the children had viewed other individuals in identical situations. Two areas of affect, aggression and self-control, were given particular attention by Bandura and Walters in their research.

Aggression is behavior intended to injure or destroy a living thing or an inanimate object. Bandura and Walters discovered that children who observe aggressive behavior are more likely to exhibit aggression in the near future than are their counterparts who observe nonaggressive behavior. Individuals who observe a model being rewarded for aggressive behavior are even more likely to imitate it. If, for example, children observe that their peers constantly fight, those children are likely to become fighters. This likelihood increases proportionately with the amount of prestige or power accrued by the fighter model in the peer group. Positive reinforcement for emitting a particular aggressive response increases the chances that this particular response will generalize to other aggressive actions. Children who often get what they want by verbal aggression may soon show an increase in hitting behavior as well. Also, the observation of aggressive behavior being rewarded in a nonsocial situation will increase the possibility that aggression will come to the foreground in a social situation. The aggressive hero who saves the day in a Western comic book becomes the model for the child's future social behavior.

The punishment of an aggressive model's behavior tends to inhibit aggressive behavior on the part of the observer, but only in the presence of the punisher. In situations where the punitive agent is not present, no decrease in the frequency of aggressive behavior is generally noted. This observer reaction is partially due to the child perceiving, in addition to the model, the equally aggressive behavior of a powerful punisher. Obviously the development of aggression is a highly complex social phenomenon.

Self-control refers to the amount of restraint individuals exercise over their personal actions. An individual may be completely self-indulgent, or completely self-denying, but most individuals fall between these two extremes. Self-indulgent individuals set personal standards for performance which are quite reasonable, and will not hesitate to lower those standards should they prove too difficult or confining. If they set a goal of two hours for study, from eight until ten o'clock, and discover that their favorite basketball team is playing a game on television at eight-thirty, self-indulgent persons will lower their study goal to a half hour. Self-denying individuals, on the other hand, set high goals for themselves which they are loath to alter. They will set a study goal of four hours and not turn on the television to watch the basketball game. Whether individuals reach for immediate gratification or for long-range gratification is indicative of a self-indulgent as opposed to a self-denying disposition, respectively. Self-indulgent students are seeking the immediate gratification of watching television. Self-denying students are seeking a long-range goal of graduation and a career.

Self-indulgence is fostered in social settings where a precarious economic or social life is the norm. The prevailing attitude in such cultures is "catch as catch can." If one hesitates, the reward will be gone. In social settings where economic and social stability is the rule, long-range goals are stressed, such as saving one's allowance for a bicycle instead of spending it on candy. Self-denying individuals are fostered by attitudes of this kind. The influence of models from within each type of social unit accounts for this phenomenon. Children who often observe a self-indulgent individual succeed or fail will tend to be or not be self-indulgent, respectively. The same is true for a child with a self-denying model. A change in self-disposition is accounted for by observing models whose dispositions differ from the observer. A self-denying child who observes a model consistently rewarded for self-indulgent behavior will become disinhibited and more self-indulgent. The converse is also true. Bandura and Walters thus conclude that the development of self-control, aggression, and other observable affective states occurs mainly through social forces.

SYNTHESIS OF AFFECTIVE DEVELOPMENT THEORIES

Erikson's psychosocial theory, Maslow's needs theory, and Bandura and Walters's social learning theory are representative of three different theoretical approaches to affective development. Each emphasizes the influence upon affective development of a different factor, either intrapsychic (Erikson), needs (Maslow), or social-psychological (Bandura and Walters). Most other affective development theories, from Freud's psychosexual theory to transactional analysis, are similarly oriented. One factor in the affective development process is stressed as being of primary importance while the other two factors are relegated to subordinate positions, or completely ignored. However, no single one of the three theoretical approaches appears able to explain all affective behaviors. Consequently, to understand the many facets involved in affective development, as presently espoused by developmental theorists, readers must not only comprehend how each of the three factors alone influences affective development, but they must also develop a framework which incorporates the effects of all three factors and their interactions. Such a framework enables individuals to recognize their own affective state and that of others. It affords them the opportunity to consciously guide affective development.

Perception is one theoretical frame of reference which incorporates all three affective factors and their interactions into a unified approach to the study of affective development. Through studying an individual's current perceptions of different situations one learns how external circumstances, internal feelings, and needs singularly and jointly influence that individual's affective behavior. Perception in this context may be conceptualized as an individual's affective synthesis of situations, for it encompasses the effects of present circumstances, present needs, and similar previous circumstances and needs.

Present needs enter perception as conscious or semiconscious goals. The individual's need state identifies the primary affective objective an individual seeks at a particular time, whether physiological satisfaction, safety, love, esteem, self-actualization, knowledge, or beauty. Present circumstances or social-psychological circumstances enter perception as information about resources available in the environment for obtaining the desired goal: whether it can be obtained through the present resources, whether those people present are likely to aid or hinder, and so forth. Similar previous circumstances and needs, or the intrapsychic state, enter perception as information about how goals have been obtained or not obtained in the past: with the voluntary aid of others, through asking for help, by one's own efforts, and so forth. Combined, these three factors of perception impose meaning and direction on individuals' interactions with their environments.

While people act in a manner meaningful to themselves from their own perspective, the purpose of their actions may not always be understood by others. For example, two seven-year-old boys both have a need for attention. One strives to receive attention by neatly doing his schoolwork, the other by being a clown. Both have the same need and the same resources in their environment. However, their past experiences are different and therefore they strive to fulfill their need in a different manner. The teacher is also a unique individual with unique perception of the situation. The teacher may recognize that the student who does schoolwork neatly desires attention, but fails to recognize that the other student also desires attention. Rather the need for self-esteem as a teacher and/or personal past experiences influence the teacher's perception. The clown may be viewed as inconsiderate and intentionally trying to irritate the teacher.

Even though recognizing that the clown desires attention, the teacher must consider the effects of paying attention to his antics. Attending to his antics adds one more experience to his repertoire of experiences in which clowning satisfied his need for attention from adults. Ignoring the student, on the other hand, results in either the student becoming frustrated because his desire for attention is unmet, or a continuation of the clowning because of the attention received from schoolmates. Obviously, the teacher must take some course of action.

Teachers and other individuals who wish to promote affective development must recognize not only an individual's current affective state, but must know how to change it and in what direction the change should take place. Playful antics performed in school may not be detrimental to a student, but later in life such behavior probably will not be appreciated by the individual's boss and co-workers. Conversely, individuals who conscientiously perform their work are likely to be appreciated. The desirable direction for affective change is indicated by the future outcomes of alternative affective states. The alternative affective state of striving for attention through conscientiously doing one's work is more likely to be beneficial to the clown in the future.

Affective development is affective change in a direction which is beneficial to the individual either socially, emotionally, or both. The process of affective development can be consciously promoted by individuals who (1) recognize affective states, (2) realize what alternative states may be more beneficial, and (3) know how to change affective states. Theories such as Maslow's needs theory, Erikson's psychosocial theory, and Bandura and Walters's social learning theory provide structural aid to individuals wishing to achieve these three insights.

The current affective state of oneself and others can be ascertained through observation and verbal interchange. Individuals' need states as reflected in their perception are manifested behaviorally by the goals they strive to attain, the activities they choose, and the actions they find satisfying. Maslow's hierarchy of needs lists the needs one might expect to detect, and delineates their order of importance for most individuals. The intrapsychic state of individuals as filtered by their perception is disclosed by their approach to a situation, their choice of possible means of attaining their goal, and their anticipation of the outcomes of their efforts. Erikson's psychosocial stages describe the various combinations of internal feelings an individual may bring to a situation. Social-psychological circumstances are situation specific, entering an individual's awareness through the individual's contact with the environment. Influential aspects of the environment are detected by the amount of attention an individual displays toward them. Bandura and Walters's social learning theory describes the characteristics of people in one's environment who are influential models.

The setting of developmental goals in the affective domain must be based on the individual's current state of development, both emotionally and socially. Answers to questions such as: "What changes would enable individuals to get along better with others? to like themselves better? to lead happier lives?" are clues to the types of change which would be beneficial. The developmental sequences outlined by Maslow and Erikson also provide valuable hints about both short-term and long-term affective goals to be considered. Fulfillment of basic needs and the positive resolution of previously negatively resolved stages and/or the currently contested stage are worthwhile affective objectives.

A change in affective state is made by altering the primary need, the intrapsychic state, and/or the social-psychological circumstances of an individual. Affective development can be induced through the favorable alteration of one or more of these three factors. Development from one need state to the next higher need state can be promoted by minimizing the dangers of proceeding to the next state and maximizing its attractiveness while simultaneously maximizing the dangers of remaining at the lower state and minimizing its attractiveness through fulfilling the essential portion of the need. A change in the need factor of affect results in the individual pursuing a different goal. To change the manner in which an individual pursues goals involves altering either the intrapsychic state or the social-psychological circumstances. Changes in these two factors usually are made jointly because changes in intrapsychic states depend upon many social-psychological experiences which do not conform to expectations based on past experiences. Social-psychological circumstances can be altered by changes in the individual's environment, or changes in the behavior of others toward the individual. Environmental changes include alterations in the real, symbolic, and representational models an individual observes, as well as changes in physical surroundings. Changes in the reactions of others toward the individual may include extreme or slight changes, obvious or subtle changes, changes involving just one person or a large group of people.

PROMOTING AFFECTIVE DEVELOPMENT THROUGH IGE

Teachers

Teachers must "have themselves together" before they can be expected to understand and promote affective development in their students. They must know their own strengths and weaknesses, understand themselves, and like themselves. They must not be motivated to teach by lower level needs for security, love, or esteem, but rather teach because teaching is a fulfilling part of their being. They must not conceive of teaching as a popularity contest or a chance for an ego trip. They must respect students whose personalities differ from their own and accept the fact that other teachers may be better able to promote the affective development of these students. They must be sensitive, conscientious individuals who view their responsibilities to students seriously.

Teachers should have the knowledge and ability to promote affective development. They should: (1) recognize current affective states, (2) realize what alternative states may be more beneficial to a student, and (3) know how to change affective states. These insights are not automatically learned in education courses, but through listening to others, being sensitive to others' feelings, and studying the affective behavior of many different people in different situations.

School Structure

IGE facilitates the control of social-psychological circumstances. In IGE schools students can be grouped in different ways according to their affective states. The size of groups, the affective characteristics of group members, the physical arrangement of groups, and the physical location of groups can be regulated. The affective characteristics of the adults who are in the class setting can be varied, allowing each student the opportunity to meet an adult with whom the student can relate.

IGE also provides for students functioning at different need states and intrapsychic states. Students who are seeking self-actualization may move freely to and from the resource center while students who need security may be placed in a group whose daily schedule is fixed. Students who are industrious and initiate projects may be allowed to plan most of their own activities, while students who wait for others to tell them what to do may be asked to choose their activities from a list of suggested activities.

Methods

IGE as applied to the affective domain specifies that teachers: (1) assess affective states, (2) work with students in setting objectives in the affective domain, and (3) plan programs to induce affective changes. These three steps are necessities in any adequate program to facilitate children's affective development. The assessment of affective states may be made through observing each student's affective behavior. More than one teacher or paraprofessional should be involved in each such assessment to prevent personal perceptions from clouding the evaluations.

For example, at Parkview Elementary School in Cedarburg, Wisconsin, an IGE school, the teachers consciously attempt to promote their children's affective development. The teachers assess current affective states through planned observation schedules and decide what beneficial changes in affective states they can foster. Last year the staff realized that the majority of their students were at Erikson's industry versus inferiority stage, Maslow's self-esteem need state, and modeled the behavior of peers and teachers. Setting as a specific schoolwide objective student growth in sensitivity to the feelings of others, they launched an IALAC campaign. The campaign began with inservice group training for the staff conducted by a guidance counselor from the community. This training program utilized group interaction exercises to promote sensitivity among teachers and between teachers and students. Meanwhile Mr. Gilpatrick, the principal, randomly placed 40 IALAC signs on students as they entered the school building in the morning. At the end of the school day the students were required to return the signs and new students were given the signs the next day. After approximately two weeks of suspense as the students attempted to guess what the letters IALAC represented, student groups were formed to talk about the meaning of these letters. IALAC is the acronym for "I Am Lovable and Capable." In the groups teachers focused the students' attention and discussion upon sensitivity to others through the analogy that when one complains to another about the other's behavior, it is like taking a chunk off that person's sign or self-esteem. If chunks of self-esteem are frequently removed, soon none is left. If this occurs day after day the person doesn't even have time to rebuild self-esteem or remake a sign, before it is taken away again. The students discussed this idea, and for the next two months made IALAC signs and wore them at school when they felt the desire or need to do so.

A general checklist which includes various need states, intrapsychic states, and social-psychological circumstances is suggested as one means of gaining an overall profile of a student's affective development. Such a checklist is useful not only in assessment, but in setting long-range instructional objectives in the affective domain. After an overall profile is obtained, behavioral observations may be made and evaluated in specific areas of affective development. Anecdotal reports are one assessment method which may aid in this evaluation and in the determination of short-term affective goals.

Students may be included in the setting of instructional objectives in the affective domain. Oftentimes they are unhappy with themselves, aware of a number of their affective weaknesses, and wish to change. Conferences with students may uncover those instructional objectives which students deem desirable and want to attain. The rapport between students and teachers should be considered when conferences are arranged. Teachers should be individuals whom students respect and trust. Tact and consideration of students' feelings should be paramount in any discussion of students' personal affective development.

Programs to induce affective development must be individually planned. Preparatory steps for controlling social-psychological experiences such as the construction of a classroom sociogram are recommended. A carefully constructed sociogram will indicate possible groupings of students and the students who may serve as possible models for other students. The satisfaction of student's basic needs may be integrated with other individualized developmental programs. By enabling students to be secure in their ability to succeed in school, by demonstrating concern for their happiness in school, by acknowledging and respecting their accomplishments, and by allowing them to choose some of their own activities, teachers minimize the attractiveness of lower level needs and maximize the possibility of all students becoming that which they are capable of being.

SUGGESTED READINGS FOR CHAPTER 5

Bandura, A. 1966. Behavioral modification through modeling procedures. In L. Krasner and L. P. Ulman (eds.), *Research in behavior modification.* New York: Holt.

The author reviews a series of laboratory studies which indicate that modeling can serve as an effective means of transmitting entire behavioral repertoires from the model to the perceiver, for disinhibiting or inhibiting existing response patterns in the perceiver, and as a means of providing discriminative or response stimuli for the perceiver. It is proposed that the achievement of successful therapeutic outcome can be accelerated through systematic use of modeling techniques whereby the individual progresses along an orderly learning sequence resulting in the final desired behavior.

Erikson, E. 1964. Eight ages of man. In C. B. Stendler (ed.), *Readings in child behavior and development*. New York: Harcourt.

Erikson proposes that human affective-psychosocial development proceeds through eight successive attitudinal stages, each of which is derived from the manner in which individuals deal with crises resulting from their attempts to meet societal demands.

Maslow, A. H. 1943. A theory of human motivation. *Psychological Review* 50: 370–396.

This article gives the reader an understanding of the early works of Maslow pertaining to the development of his theory of motivation. In it he formulates his positive theory which he believed satisfied theoretical, clinical, observational, and experimental demands. The article provides for the reader Maslow's suggested program for future research on the subject of motivation.

REFERENCES

Bandura, A. 1966. Behavioral modification through modeling procedures. In L. Krasner and L. P. Ullman (eds.), *Research in behavior modification*. New York: Holt.

———, and W. Mischel 1965. Modification of self-imposed delay of reward through exposure to live and symbolic models. *Journal of Personality and Social Psychology* 2: 698–705.

———, and R. Walters 1963. *Social learning and personality development*. New York: Holt.

Elkind, D. 1970. Erik Erikson's eight ages of man. *The New York Times Magazine,* April. Reprinted 1973 in *Annual editions: readings in human development '73–'74*. Guilford, Conn.: Dushkin Publishing.

Erikson, E. 1950. *Childhood and society*. New York: Norton.

——— 1964. Eight ages of man. In C. B. Stendler (ed.), *Readings in child behavior and development*. New York: Harcourt.

Holte, D. L. 1971. Published quotation. Campbell, Calif.: John Philip.

Maslow, A. H. 1943. A theory of human motivation. *Psychological Review* 50: 370–396.

——— 1968a. Personality problems and personality growth. In D. E. Hamacheck (ed.), *Human dynamics in psychology and education*. Boston: Allyn and Bacon.

——— 1968b. *Toward a psychology of being*. (2nd ed.) New York: Van Nostrand.

——— 1970. *Motivation and personality*. (2nd ed.) New York: Harper & Row.

6

Moral
Development

Objectives

Upon completion of this chapter, the reader should be able:

- To identify character education and moral relativism as the approaches to moral development traditionally used in schools.

- To understand Piaget's conceptualization of moral development and differentiate among the premoral period, the morality of constraint stage, and the morality of cooperation stage.

- To understand Kohlberg's conceptualization of moral development and differentiate among the premoral period, and the hierarchy of levels of morality:

  a. Preconventional level
     1) Punishment and obedience (Stage 1)
     2) Instrumental-relativist (Stage 2)
  b. Conventional level
     1) Interpersonal concordance (Stage 3)
     2) Law-and-order (Stage 4)
  c. Postconventional level
     1) Social contract, legalistic (Stage 5)
     2) Universal-ethical principle (Stage 6)

- To describe the ways that moral development may be facilitated by instructional programming for the individual student.

*Youths who understand justice act more justly, and the man who understands justice helps create a moral climate which goes far beyond his immediate and personal acts. The universal society is the beneficiary.**

Lawrence Kohlberg

THEORIES OF MORAL DEVELOPMENT

It was final exam day in Miss Smith's senior English literature class. Judy had studied for this exam for weeks. She needed a passing grade on this test in order to graduate. She needed a high school diploma in order to meet the employment requirements for the typing pool at Brown, Inc., a firm which had agreed to employ her beginning the week after graduation. Miss Smith handed out the exams. Judy glanced at the test and immediately realized she had not studied the particular details that Miss Smith asked on the test. Sally, Judy's best friend, was sitting in the desk next to Judy. Sally was exceptionally competent in English literature. Realizing Judy's predicament, Sally indicated to Judy that she would help her pass the test. Judy copied enough answers from Sally's paper to pass and graduate.

Moral judgments and decisions do not occur in a vacuum but rather in a world in which very little is perfectly right or perfectly wrong. Many gray areas exist. In the above case, what should Judy have done? Is Judy wrong for copying? Is Sally wrong for allowing Judy to copy? Is Miss Smith wrong for not making the content of what she would place on this exam clear? Is the school system wrong for requiring a passing grade in English literature for graduation? Is Brown, Inc. wrong for requiring a high school diploma for employment in its typing pool?

Answers to questions like these have been attempted by many developmental theorists in assessing and explaining moral development, and by many school personnel in planning a moral development curriculum. Until the 1920s teaching specific moral and societal values was considered one of the primary functions of schools. Character education, in which certain community values were emphasized in school materials and student relations, was the curriculum used in most schools. This type of curriculum is also termed the "bag-of-vir-

---

* From *Psychology Today* magazine, Sept. 1968. Copyright © Ziff-Davis Publishing Company. All rights reserved.

tues" approach, because it emphasized various traits such as those presently listed by the Boy Scouts and the Boys' Clubs.

Hartshorne and May (1928–30) studied the effects of this type of curriculum on moral conduct. Neither participants in character-education classes nor religious instruction programs were found to have a higher level of moral conduct than nonparticipants. This study, together with the popularity of Freud's notion (1938) that moral and personal values were fixed by the age of five, led to a decrease in the use of the character education approach to moral development.

During the latter portion of this century, some communities have attempted to reestablish the character education curriculum in their community. However, while most community members are in agreement concerning the abstract virtues such as neatness and perseverance, which they wish students to value, these communities have met with difficulty when trying to define the virtues their members hold in common. What is the difference between stubbornness and perseverence? Do long hair, faded jeans, or T-shirts which are not tucked in mean a student isn't neat? Because of educational research and the problem of defining virtues, the character education approach has some serious limitations as a moral development curriculum.

A second approach to moral development in schools became popular as an alternative to character education. This approach is known as moral relativism. It is based on the assumption that the teaching of specific values is the duty of a student's family. The school may operate according to a set of societal values, but these values are not to be conceived of or presented as better or worse than any other value system. The respect for authority approach and the student's social adjustment approach are two examples of this type of value system. In the first, the school emphasizes respect for its rules, regardless of whether they are agreed upon by all. In its extreme, it could foster a nation like Germany during World War II in which respect for authority was considered to be the supreme value. In the second, the school emphasizes the ability of a student to interact in a socially acceptable way. This approach, while stressing the importance of the student in the developmental process, also has its limitations. In its extreme, the students who do not conform to what the teacher designates as socially acceptable behavior, no matter what the reason, are forced to change their behavior. Students who are frustrated because they do not comprehend a task, and become aggressive, are forced to change the outlet of their frustration even though the cause of their unacceptable behavior may still exist.

Either some form of character education or moral relativism is the approach to moral development presently used in today's schools. However, both forms have some serious limitations. Recent research in the area of moral development has resulted in another approach which is being experimentally conducted in a number of schools with significant results. This approach is a refinement of Piaget's theory of moral development.

PIAGET'S CONCEPTUALIZATION OF MORAL DEVELOPMENT

Assumptions Basic to Piaget's Theory

Piaget (1965) views one's moral values as particular attitudes toward the duties and rights of individuals. Moral development, according to Piaget, constitutes a directional change in one's attitude toward rules and justice, resulting from one's ability to view situations objectively. Thus, Piaget approaches moral development from his cognitive-stage theoretical orientation. He assumes that certain cognitive processes are necessary for moral development to occur, and that moral development occurs in an ordered series of stages.

Piaget postulates that children enter the world with certain innate primitive attitudes and concepts, such as the need to organize and integrate their experiences, and also with a primitive sense of justice. These attitudes and concepts are not exhibited until children begin to interact in their environment. Consequently, prior to the occurrence of a particular moral attitude, Piaget assumes the existence of a pre-moral level of development.

The occurrence of moral development, accordance to Piaget, encompasses two stages. These stages are distinguished from each other by the basic attitude toward the world which they encompass. This attitude is cognitive in nature and directly related to children's perception of the world. Thus, children who are egocentric and subjective differ in moral development from older children who are objective and able to view a situation from another's point of view.

Piaget assumes that changes in cognitive development and moral development cannot be separated. When children's perception of their world changes, their attitude toward rules and justice also changes. This change, Piaget assumes, happens in all areas of moral development at once, rather than gradually in the particular areas of moral values with which the child is most familiar.

Since Piaget's moral development theory, like his cognitive development theory, is based on the unfolding of children's innate tendencies as they interact in their environment, parents and teachers have a limited role in fostering moral development. Piaget suggests that the less interference in the natural developmental process imposed on children, the more likely the occurrence of children's development at the predetermined time. Thus parents and teachers should avoid hindering this natural process by not curtailing experiences through rules children are unable to comprehend.

The overall affective component of moral development, as conceived by Piaget, is respect. Children's respect for their parents and other authoritarian figures gradually evolves through their interaction with others, to respect for their peers and society in general. Therefore, Piaget emphasizes the responsibility of authority figures to be suitable recipients of respect.

Piaget's Stages of Moral Development

Piaget delineates two stages of moral development, based on moral reasoning. Preceding these stages is a premoral period, similar to the sensorimotor period of his cognitive development theory, during which rules do not exist for children. They are unable to remember from one moment to the next, and therefore, rules, as such, are not a part of their life space. When given marbles to play with, children in the premoral period will not attempt to play with them according to social rules. Rather, they will use the marbles as free-play material, imposing on this play situation certain generalized methods of play such as throwing, sucking, and so forth. These generalized methods of play, called motor rules, differ from social or moral rules because they are solitary in nature, not based on facilitating interaction with others, and involve trial-and-error usage of an object. Likewise, during this premoral period, the imposition of rules such as Mother saying "No" is thwarted because of children's inability to remember. Children will "forget" within a short period of time, and again attempt the prohibited deed.

Morality of Constraint Stage

Following the premoral period is Piaget's first stage called the morality of constraint stage. This stage begins at about the age of speech and can be observed in young children's imitation of the social, rulebound play of older children. Initially (approximately age three to five) this play is enacted in solitude, often within visual sight of older children. Therefore, it is often termed parallel play. Later (approximately age five to eight), children can be observed in play situations with others. This play is governed by social and mutually accepted rules. However, oftentimes these rules are vague and unknowingly broken. This stage of moral development lasts until about seven to nine years of age.

The outstanding characteristic of the morality of constraint stage is the children's perception of adults as being all-powerful and all-knowing. The children accept without question the rules and judgments given by adults. This unconditional respect for adults, together with young children's inability to distinguish between the subjective and objective components of their experiences, leads to a conception of rules as being absolute and sacred. Children at this stage of moral development believe that all rules were created by parents or some authority figure such as God. When alternative rules to a game are suggested, these children adamantly defend the existent rules. New rules are considered unfair, even if they are mutually accepted by all.

Other predominant characteristics of this stage of moral development include moral realism, a belief in immanent justice and an expiatory orientation toward punishment. These characteristics reflect the perceptual organization and cognitive thought present in children during this time. In particular, egocentricism and subjective realism are indicated. Children view themselves as the center of all activity, they do not realize that others may have a different view of a particular situation, and they are unable to separate their own feelings or possible feelings from a situation. Egocentricism and subjective realism combine with children's supreme respect for adults to create a particular moral attitude.

Moral realism is one characteristic of this attitude. It is a belief that acts should be judged on the basis of their material consequences, rather than on the intention behind the act. A child exhibiting moral realism (Piaget 1965) would judge a girl who made a big hole in her dress while trying to make her mother a nice surprise as naughtier than a girl who made a small hole in her dress while playing with scissors when she wasn't supposed to be playing with scissors. Likewise, a boy who steals a roll for a starving friend is considered naughtier than a girl who steals a less expensive item for herself. Moral realism is expressed not only in moral judgment, but also in moral reasoning. A lie is defined by the moral realist as an untrue statement, regardless of the intention. Its seriousness is as great as its deviation from the truth. A boy who explains a lost schoolbook as being taken by a monster, when his imagination has convinced him that this is true is naughtier than another boy who explains the lost schoolbook as being stolen when it actually wasn't. In addition, the moral realist believes that exposure of a misdeed adds to its wrongness. A lie which fails to deceive is naughtier than one which is undetected. A boy whose schoolbook was taken by a monster is more likely to have his exaggeration detected. This child then has compounded the seriousness of his act by his inability to deceive successfully.

Immanent justice is a second characteristic of a child's moral attitude at the morality of constraint stage. It is a belief that all wrong acts will eventually be punished, and that the punishment will be directly caused by the wrongful act. A girl steals apples from an orchard. While she is crossing the plank spanning the creek between her home and the orchard, the plank breaks. The girl believes that the plank broke because she stole the apples. She believes that if she had not stolen the apples, the plank would not have broken.

A belief in expiatory punishment is a third characteristic of a child's moral attitude at the morality of constraint stage. Expiatory punishment is based on atonement through suffering. Expiatory punishment for an offense need not be related to the offense, but it should be as painful as the offense is serious. Spanking a boy for refusing to clean his room differs from confining him to his room until it is cleaned. Spanking in this context is expiatory punishment. If the room is twice as dirty as the last time the child refused to clean it, an expiatory approach to punishment would dictate that the child should be spanked twice as hard, or twice as many times. The child who was at the morality of constraint stage would then feel that the parent was just, and that the child had made atonement for the offense.

Morality of Cooperation Stage

Piaget's second stage of moral development is called the morality of cooperation stage. Children at the beginning of this stage (approximately age 7 to 9) completely understand rules and obey them to the letter. Shortly thereafter (approximately age 11 to 12), rules themselves become objects to manipulate and the child begins to revise them and elaborate on them.

The outstanding characteristic of the morality of cooperation stage is children's perception of social order. They realize that the society in which they live is based on cooperation, mutual respect, and equality. Rules are no longer regarded as sacred, but changeable provided that others agree to accept the new rules.

Other predominant characteristics of this stage of moral development include moral relativism, a belief in restitution, and a reciprocity orientation toward punishment. These characteristics are reflective of a new stage in perceptual organization and cognitive thought. Children are now able to perceive and consider the point of view of other individuals. They are able to separate their own feelings from a situation, and contemplate the situation in an objective manner. These abilities create a new moral attitude.

Moral relativism is one characteristic of this attitude. It is a belief that both the intentions and material consequences of an act should be considered in judging an act. The spirit rather than the letter of the law is important. The child exhibiting moral relativism (Piaget 1965) would judge the girl who made a big hole in her dress while trying to make her mother a nice surprise as less naughty than a girl who made a small hole in her dress while playing with scissors when she wasn't supposed to be playing with them. Likewise, the boy who stole a roll for a starving friend is less naughty than a girl who stole a less expensive item for herself. Moral relativism is expressed not only in moral judgment but also in moral reasoning. A lie is defined by the moral relativist as an untrue statement made with an intent to deceive. The boy who believed his schoolbook was taken by a monster is not intentionally distorting the truth, and therefore is not lying.

A belief in restitution is a second characteristic of children's moral attitude at the morality of cooperation stage. No longer do children think all their wrongful acts will be discovered and punished. Rather, it is the individuals' moral responsibility to compensate others for the harm they do to them. A girl at this stage of moral development who steals apples from an orchard and later the plank spanning the creek between her home and the orchard breaks as she is crossing it, does not believe that the plank broke because she stole the apples. Her getting wet does not compensate for her act of stealing. She still has the moral responsibility to compensate in some way the owner of the orchard for the stolen apples.

Punishment by reciprocity is a third characteristic of a child's moral attitude at the morality of cooperation stage. Reciprocal punishment is based on atonement through restitution. Reciprocal punishment for an offense is directly related to the nature of the offense and the offender's breach of other's trust. Confining a child to a room until it is cleaned is one type of reciprocal punishment. It is directly related to the offense, an unclean room, and is aimed at rectifying the child's original shirking of responsibility. Reciprocal punishment, unlike expiatory punishment, does not have to be as painful as the offense is serious. Rather it is governed by the logical consequences of the offense. If a child's room is twice as dirty as last time, the child does not have to spend twice as long confined to the room. The child regulates the time period by being quick or slow in cleaning the room. Likewise, the child believes intentions and possible mitigating circumstances should be considered in the application of this type of punishment. If the room was not cleaned because the child was ill, or had to help a parent that day, the child feels a time extension or assistance in cleaning the room should be given. The child at the reciprocal punishment level of moral development believes the punishment is just if it logically fits the offense, and if all mitigating circumstances are considered and discussed before punishment.

While Piaget's observations of the moral development of children in Switzerland lead to his postulating a specific sequence of developmental stages, he is careful in interpreting these observations. The ages at which these stages occur overlap considerably, and individual differences are quite prevalent. He also suggests that different cultures and populations will yield moral development patterns that are somewhat different from those of children in Switzerland. Teachers should be aware of the high probability of many individual differences in moral development in children in their units. Piaget's stages should be viewed as a guideline to ascertaining each child's level of moral development, rather than as a method of dividing a class into two moral development groups.

KOHLBERG'S CONCEPTUALIZATION OF MORAL DEVELOPMENT

Assumptions Basic to Kohlberg's Theory

Kohlberg's theory of moral development is a modification of Piaget's theory (Kohlberg 1971a, Peters 1971). Research based on Piaget's theory resulted in the discovery of a number of fallacies in the theory. Kohlberg modified Piaget's theory to conform to research results, while also expanding the theory. Kohlberg's moral development theory is thus both similar to and different from Piaget's theory.

Like Piaget, Kohlberg views moral development from a cognitive-stage approach. He assumes that one of the major components of moral development is the way in which individuals have organized their perceptions of the world. As this cognitive organization becomes more complex, individuals become more capable of higher stages of moral development. Kohlberg therefore assumes that moral development occurs in an ordered sequence of stages.

Kohlberg, like Piaget, also postulates that children enter the world with certain primitive attitudes and concepts such as the need to organize and integrate their experiences, and also with a primitive sense of justice. These attitudes and concepts toward moral development are not exhibited until children begin to interact in their environment. Consequently, prior to the occurrence of a particular moral attitude, Kohlberg assumes the existence of a premoral level of development.

The occurrence of moral development, according to Kohlberg, encompasses three different levels, each composed of two stages. Kohlberg's moral development theory thus contains six stages altogether. The three levels of Kohlberg's moral development theory are distinguished from each other by the source of value upon which they focus. The stages within each level are distinguished from each other by the particular aspects of the value upon which they focus. Children's unique perception and understanding of the world, the cognitive component of moral development, is directly related to the level of moral development that is possible for them to achieve. However, not all children reach the moral development level that is possible for them to achieve.

At Kohlberg's preconventional level children focus on themselves as the major source of value.

Kohlberg, like Piaget, assumes that cognitive development is a necessary component of moral development. Unlike Piaget, Kohlberg holds that cognitive development does not completely coincide with moral development. Children must be at a particular stage of cognitive development to achieve a particular stage of moral development, but because they are at a particular stage of cognitive development does not mean they are at a particular stage of moral development. Their moral development stage could be any stage at or below that which coincides with their cognitive development stage.

Likewise, Kohlberg differs from Piaget concerning the nature of change in moral development. Kohlberg postulates that changes in moral development occur gradually, with the particular areas of moral values with which children are most familiar being the first areas to change. Therefore children can be between stages, with the stage which describes the majority of their thinking designated as their stage of moral development.

Kohlberg's moral development theory is based on children's innate, primitive concept of justice and their innate tendencies to organize their perceptions and to interact with their environment. Kohlberg emphasizes the role of interaction in promoting moral development. He assumes that persons of normal intelligence can achieve their highest stage of moral development if they are given the opportunity to interact with other individuals of varying viewpoints. Parents and teachers can thus not only allow children to develop but can also foster moral development through providing the child with opportunities to interact.

Kohlberg's Levels of Moral Development

Kohlberg delineates three levels of moral development with two stages present at each level. Individuals' stage of moral development on Kohlberg's hierarchy is determined by the reasoning processes they use in making moral judgments, not the moral judgment itself. Thus, Kohlberg claims that two individuals can be at the same stage of moral development, although one judges an act as right and the other judges the same act as wrong.

Preceding the beginning of Kohlberg's moral development stages is a premoral period which Kohlberg assumes to be identical with the premoral period of Piaget. Following this premoral period are Kohlberg's moral development levels and stages. Each level emphasizes a different source of value, i.e., physical well-being, harmony with society, or justice. The two stages within each level emphasize different aspects of the value i.e., physical well-being can be viewed in terms of physical punishment or physical rewards.

Preconventional Level

The first level of Kohlberg's hierarchy is called the preconventional level of moral development. At this level individuals focus on themselves as the major source of value. This level is divided into two stages. The first stage is called the punishment and obedience stage, and the second is called the instrumental-relativist stage. In each stage individuals judge their actions according to the actions' concrete effects upon themselves. At the first stage, individuals distinguish between actions that are punished and actions which are not punished. An act is wrong if it is punished. At the second stage, individuals make a distinction between acts which are not punished and those which are rewarded. An act is wrong if it is not rewarding in some concrete way.

An example (Kohlberg 1969b, Kohlberg and Turiel 1971) of an individual's moral reasoning at this level of moral development is the individual's response to the story of Heinz, who is unable to obtain an expensive drug to prolong the life of his wife and hence steals it. The individual at the punishment and obedience stage (the first stage) may respond that Heinz was right to steal because he would be punished by his relatives if he did not steal. Likewise, an individual at this stage may respond that Heinz was wrong to steal the drug because he will be punished by the law for stealing it. The individual at the instrumental-relativist stage (the second stage) may respond that Heinz was right to steal the drug because he would have his wife after he got out of jail. Likewise, an individual at this stage (the second stage) may respond that Heinz was wrong to steal the drug because his wife will die before he is released from jail.

In this story, each individual is required to judge the act of stealing from the perspective of Heinz. The individual whose moral reasoning is dominated by whether stealing or nonstealing is punished is at the punishment and obedience stage (the first stage). The individual whose moral reasoning is dominated by whether stealing or nonstealing is rewarded is at the instrumental-relativist stage (the second stage). The responses made are at the preconventional level because they focus on the value of stealing or not stealing in terms of the physical self.

Conventional Level

The second level of Kohlberg's hierarchy is called the conventional level of moral development. At this level individuals focus on social harmony as the major source of value. This level is divided into the interpersonal concordance (the third stage) and the law-and-order stage (the fourth stage). In each stage individuals judge their actions according to whether the actions agree with social rules and laws. At the third stage, individuals distinguish between actions that are favored by others in their immediate social sphere, and those that are not favored. At the fourth stage, individuals distinguish between actions that are favored by their society's law and those that are not favored.

Using the story of Heinz stealing a drug to prolong the life of his wife produces different responses at this level and at these stages than were made at the preconventional level. The individual at the interpersonal concordance stage (the third stage) may respond that Heinz was right to steal because his family would approve. Likewise, an individual at this stage may respond that Heinz was wrong to steal the drug because he will bring dishonor upon his family by stealing. The individual at the law-and-order stage (the fourth stage) may respond that Heinz was right to steal the drug because it is his duty through marriage. Likewise, an individual at this stage may respond that Heinz was wrong to steal the drug because stealing is against the law.

Individuals whose moral reasoning is dominated by whether stealing is favored by their families are at the interpersonal concordance stage (the third stage). The individual whose moral reasoning is dominated by whether stealing or not stealing is favored by societal laws is at the law-and-order stage (the fourth stage). The responses made are at the conventional level because they focus upon the value of stealing or not stealing in terms of social rules and laws, not personal well-being as at the preconventional level. These responses differ from those made at the preconventional level because of their emphasis on the opinions of members of the individual's society, rather than the physical consequences of the individual's decision.

Postconventional Level

The third level of Kohlberg's hierarchy is called the postconventional level of moral development. At this level of moral development individuals focus on justice as the major source of value. This level is divided into the social contract, legalistic stage (the fifth stage) and the universal-ethical principle stage (the sixth stage). In each stage individuals judge their actions according to the actions' agreement with their privileges and duties as members of society. At the fifth stage, individuals view their membership in a social order as obligatory and most important. They distinguish between actions that are favored by the spirit of their society's laws even though specific laws may at times contradict these actions, and those actions that are not basic to their society. At the sixth stage individuals view their membership in the human race as obligatory and most important. They distinguish between actions that are basic to the well-being of all people and those that are basic to the well-being of only a select portion of the populace.

Using the story of Heinz once again produces different responses at this level and at these stages than were made at either the preconventional or conventional levels. The individual at the social contract, legalistic stage (the fifth stage) may respond that Heinz was right to steal the drug because the decision is based on the individual's society's value for life. Likewise, an individual at this stage may respond that Heinz was wrong to steal the drug because the decision is contrary to the individual's society's values, i.e., respect for property is more valuable in the individual's society than life, and Heinz's obligation to his society dictates that he must uphold this social value. The individual at the universal-ethical principle stage (the sixth stage) may respond that Heinz was right to steal the drug because a human life is more important than property. Likewise, the individual at this stage may respond that Heinz was wrong to steal the drug because he jeopardized his own life and the lives of others during the act of stealing.

The individual whose moral reasoning is dominated by whether stealing or not stealing is favored by the values, but perhaps not the laws, of his society is at the social contract, legalistic stage (the fifth stage). The individual whose moral reasoning is dominated by whether stealing or not stealing is more beneficial to mankind is at the universal-ethical principle stage (the sixth stage). The responses made are at the postconventional level because they focus on the value of stealing or not stealing in terms of individual rights and duties, not social rules or physical well-being. They differ from responses made at the conventional and preconventional levels because of their emphasis on the rights and responsibilities of an individual, rather than accordance with the dictates of others or physical consequences.

These six stages of moral development have been observed by Kohlberg (1969b) in middle- and lower-class urban boys residing in the United States and Britain, as well as preliterate and semiliterate villages in Taiwan, Mexico, and Turkey. Although differences in the age at which certain stages are attained were observed, as well as differences in the number of individuals who reach the higher stages of his hierarchy, Kohlberg found that these six stages exist in all cultures and develop in the same sequence. The moral reasoning of children in the United States was found to change from the preconventional to the conventional level between the ages of approximately 10 to 13, and from the conventional to the postconventional level between the ages of approximately 15 and 19 (Kohlberg and Turiel

1971). Thus, Kohlberg suggests it is during the child's school years that moral development is fostered and achieved.

PIAGET AND KOHLBERG COMPARED

Piaget and Kohlberg both approach moral development from a cognitive-stage orientation. While Piaget postulates the existence of two stages and Kohlberg the existence of six stages, both believe that certain cognitive processes are necessary for moral development to occur, and that moral development occurs in a sequence of ordered stages. Piaget's moral development stages correspond with his cognitive development stages: the premoral period occurring at approximately the same age as the sensorimotor period; the morality of constraint period occurring at approximately the same age as the preoperations period; and the morality of cooperation period occurring at approximately the same age as concrete operations. Kohlberg's moral development levels are based on attainment of a certain stage in Piaget's cognitive-developmental hierarchy (Kohlberg 1971a). The child must have attained the preoperational stage to achieve Kohlberg's preconventional level; concrete operations to achieve Kohlberg's conventional level; and formal operations to achieve Kohlberg's postconventional level. Thus, although both Piaget and Kohlberg have a cognitive-stage theory of moral development, Piaget assumes that moral development occurs in conjunction with cognitive development, whereas Kohlberg assumes that moral development can occur if cognitive development occurs, but that moral development does not necessarily occur in conjunction with cognitive development. Piaget would agree that all children at a high stage of cognitive development are at a high stage of moral development. Kohlberg would state that while all children at a high stage of moral development are at a high stage of cognitive development, not all children at a high stage of cognitive development are at a high stage of moral development.

Piaget and Kohlberg also approach changes in moral reasoning ability from a different point of view. Piaget postulates that a change from one to another of his stages happens all at once, in all areas of moral concern. Kohlberg postulates that a gradual change from one to another of his stages happens, with the areas of moral concern with which the individual is most familiar being the first to change. Research (MacRae 1954, Johnson 1962) concerning this difference using Piaget's initial methods suggests that a gradual change does occur. Kohlberg (1969b) has found that typically only about 50 percent of a child's moral judgment is at one stage, with the remainder distributed one stage above and one stage below this dominant stage. In older adolescents and adults a higher percentage of moral judgments are at one stage, but use of the adjoining stages still occurs.

Piaget and Kohlberg also differ in terms of the age range in which they believe moral development occurs. Piaget's observations of Swiss children led to his hypothesis of moral development occurring between birth and approximately 12 years of age. Kohlberg's observations (1970) led to his hypothesis of moral development occurring between birth and the mid-twenties in an individual's life. Research concerning this difference (Kohlberg 1964, Mussen 1969), using Piaget's initial methods, suggests that Piaget underestimates the age range in which moral development occurs. Because Kohlberg's method of assessing moral development differs from Piaget's method, the results of this research do not verify Kohlberg's estimate of age range. However, throughout Kohlberg's studies of various cultures and populations, the range of birth to mid-twenties appears consistent.

The methods with which Piaget and Kohlberg assess moral development may account for some of their differences. Piaget observes children at play and presents pairs of stories which represent different moral judgment criteria, asking questions of the children once the preferred story is determined. The stories of the two girls who cut holes in their dresses, and the children who stole articles are examples of these story pairs. Kohlberg presents one story involving a moral decision and asks the individual to explain the moral reasoning the individual used in reaching a decision. The story of Heinz is an example of this type of story. In evaluating the stage of moral reasoning from the individual's explanations of moral decisions, different criteria are also used by Piaget and Kohlberg. Kohlberg's criteria are more than twice as numerous as Piaget's and include all of Piaget's criteria. These differences in moral development assessment are important differences in understanding and applying Piaget and Kohlberg in the school.

The differences in extensiveness of research between Piaget and Kohlberg are also important. Piaget's theory of moral development was based on middle-class Swiss children. He suggests that it should be applied with care in other cultures and socioeconomic groups. Differences in both pattern of development, types of individual differences, and rate of development may occur. Kohlberg's theory of moral development has been applied in various cultures and socioeconomic groups including middle- and lower-class Americans. It has been found to be applicable to all groups studied, although rate of development and average final stage attainment varies (Kohlberg and Turiel 1971). These differences should be recognized in the development and implementation of a moral development curriculum.

Kohlberg and Piaget both assume that children are born with innate tendencies to organize and integrate their experiences, and also with a primitive sense of justice. Piaget emphasizes the natural unfolding of these innate characteristics through the children's freedom to interact with their environment, free from interferences from parents and teachers. Kohlberg emphasizes the necessity of the interactional experiences in the development of these innate tendencies through optimal structuring of children's experiences. Research (Kohlberg 1971b) using a discussion method and Kohlberg's assessment method suggests that moral development can be fostered through structured experiences, and that this development is maintained into the future. Whether these structured experiences foster moral development, or merely eliminate interference in moral development, is unknown. However, it is known that certain classroom experiences coincide with gains in moral development.

STIMULATING MORAL DEVELOPMENT IN THE IGE SCHOOL

Theory

Both Piaget and Kohlberg assume that children are born with innate tendencies which unfold or develop through interactional experiences. While the importance of interactional experiences for moral development is viewed differently by Kohlberg and Piaget, both advocate a natural environment which allows these experiences. Individually Guided Education may provide such a natural environment. It allows students to organize and integrate their many experiences in interacting with one another and with several adults. In this way there is interaction with persons at stages both higher and lower than the particular individual student.

The research of Hartshorne and May (1928–30) concerning the influence of character education suggests that direct teaching of moral principles does not foster a higher level of moral development. Kohlberg (1971a) believes that the understanding of cognitive principles cannot be directly taught. Since both types of understanding involve a gradual reordering of cognitive processes, Kohlberg advocates the use of discovery methods to stimulate moral growth. Using this method Kohlberg (1971b) conducted a number of classes in moral reasoning. Both teacher-led discussion groups and student groups were used, with groups being formed of students in adjacent stages of moral development. Results of this study indicate that students exposed to a discovery method of moral education have a significant increase in their moral reasoning ability. Retesting a year later showed that this increase in ability had been retained by the students. The discovery method thus appears to foster moral development.

The stimulation of moral development through the presentation of moral reasoning one stage above the student's current stage of reasoning is an essential consideration in Kohlberg's method. Since fifty percent of a child's reasoning is at one stage with the remainder occupying the adjacent stages, the child has some understanding of this higher stage. Kohlberg hypothesizes that through stimulating this understanding, the gradual reordering process is hastened and moral development occurs.

Another essential consideration in applying Kohlberg's method is to focus on the moral reasoning exhibited by students, not the decision itself. A decision that a particular act is right or wrong can be made for many different reasons, at many different stages. It is these reasons that are important, and denote the student's moral developmental stage. It is an advancement in this reasoning ability that is of concern.

Roblee (1973) states that seven basic steps are necessary in teaching moral education curriculum:

1. Ascertain the student's present stage of moral reasoning (Kohlberg and Turiel 1971).

2. Stimulate the student's use of his current stage of moral reasoning (Kohlberg 1964).

3. Present the student with dilemmas emphasizing moral reasoning one stage above his reasoning level that can't easily be solved with his present stage of reasoning (Kohlberg 1964, Kohlberg and Turiel 1971).

4. Allow the student time to consider and discuss these dilemmas (Kohlberg 1970).

5. Point out inconsistencies and inadequacies in the student's reasoning process (Kohlberg 1970, Kohlberg and Turiel 1971).

6. Encourage logical resolution of these inconsistencies and inadequacies (Kohlberg and Turiel 1971).

7. Foster awareness of the adequacies of the 'higher' stage of moral reasoning in the current dilemmas and in other situations (Kohlberg and Turiel 1971).

These seven basic steps can be related to instructional programming for the individual student and thereby to fostering moral values in school-age children in IGE schools. The first two steps relate to initial assessment. The instructional objective set for each student is to progress to the next higher stage. Steps 3 through 7 relate to the planning and implementation of an instructional program. In addition, Step 7 provides for subsequent assessment through observation by unit teachers.

The assessment of the student's present level of moral reasoning and stimulating its development to higher stages then are the important phases of Kohlberg's moral education curriculum. Assessment of the student's current stage of functioning can be made in a number of ways. Teachers of an instructional and research unit can require their students to explain their resolutions of Piaget's story pairs or of Kohlberg's moral dilemmas. They can discuss with the students possible resolutions of real moral conflicts, or they can observe the students' social interactions. At age seven and above, repetitive stealing and bullying are indicators of moral immaturity of judgment. For older students, their actions in situations where cheating and lying are possible are predictive of their moral judgment level. For still older students, their actions in political dilemmas are related to their level of moral development.

Stimulation of development, the other important phase of Kohlberg's moral education curriculum, involves instructional materials, classroom activities, and teaching. Instructional materials for moral education classes encompass a wide range of topics. Current classroom situations of moral conflict and Kohlberg's ten hypothetical dilemmas are suitable for children of all ages. Piaget's story pairs and discussions of various occupations, in terms of the reason for their selection and the degree of social respect each engenders, have been found to be morally instructive for younger children. For older children, public issues, such as found in the Oliver public-political dilemmas, have been found to be effective instructional tools (Kohlberg 1971b).

A number of different instructional activities can be used to complement the instructional materials available. Small group discussions among students in adjacent stages, or teacher-led discussions, are one possibility. Role playing in which each student dramatizes the feelings and attitudes of a number of different characters in a particular moral situation is a second possibility. Literature in which the characters present moral reasoning at one stage above the reader's dominant stage is a third possibility. Many other activities formulated for the needs of particular students will become apparent to the thoughtful, creative teacher.

The teachers are the most constant element of a moral development curriculum. Whether a specific moral education curriculum is

Role playing is one method of fostering moral development.

being taught or not, teachers' decisions and reasoning are present at all times. To effectively foster moral development, teachers must handle unit management problems in a manner their students will understand, yet differently from the way they would handle moral problems, so as not to confuse the two in the minds of their students. Too often this difference is not evident, and students think it is morally wrong to whisper in class or to have a messy desk. In dealing with moral problems, teachers must know the moral stage of each of their students, and approach moral problems in the unit at a level which the particular student can understand. Too often teachers use either too low a level of moral reasoning, which causes rejection by the student, or too high a level of moral reasoning, which is incomprehensible to the student and consequently ignored.

Application

The application of this moral education curriculum in IGE is regulated by the seven basic steps. The teachers of elementary school, middle school, and junior high school can direct their actions and programs through the use of these steps.

Elementary School Grades

Most elementary school children will be at the preconventional level of Kohlberg's hierarchy, and between Piaget's morality of constraint and morality of cooperation stages. Teachers should begin their moral education program by assessing the current stage of each of their students.

They may begin in the elementary school units by assessing the position of their students through individual or small-group discussions with their students of Piaget's story pairs, observing the reasoning used by each of their students. Jimmy, a student in Mrs. Jones's primary unit, quickly expressed his reasoning and decision concerning the stories of the boy who stole the roll for a friend, and the girl who stole a hair ribbon for herself. Jimmy thought the girl's act was not as wrong as the boy's act, but added that the boy was doing it for a better reason and his friend would remember his kindness. Mrs. Jones, wishing to explore Jimmy's reasoning in this situation, asked him what he would do if he was the father of these children. Jimmy answered that each child would have to pay the storekeeper for the article they stole. Mrs. Jones through these statements decided that Jimmy was between Piaget's two stages of moral development, because he did recognize intentionality and logical consequences, but did not alter his judgment of the seriousness of the acts nor the severity of the punishment. The boy in the story was naughtier and would have to pay more. Likewise, Mrs. Jones decided Jimmy was between Kohlberg's punishment and obedience stage and his instrumental relativist stage because of Jimmy's consideration of the friend's loyalty to the boy in the story.

Since Jimmy was an active, outgoing boy who learned through listening and doing, Mrs. Jones decided to place him in a small discussion and role-playing group with a variety of her other students who were in or between these stages of the moral development hierarchies. This group was working on an occupations project in conjunction with a reading and social studies project. Together, these students discussed the jobs of various people such as firemen and policemen. Their goal was to portray the services each performed in a typical day. The group was to include such activities as directing traffic for policemen and fire prevention inspections for firemen.

Through the portrayal of these activities, the group would focus on the self-rewards gained by helping others, and thus would learn to judge actions from this perspective.

The Middle School

Middle school children should be in the process of changing from Kohlberg's preconventional level to his conventional level. In this group of students, teachers can expect to find the first four stages of Kohlberg's hierarchy because of differences in rate of moral development among students. Most of these students will also be at Piaget's morality of cooperation stage, although exceptions may be present. Again, teachers should begin their moral education program by assessing the current stage of each of their students.

They may begin in the middle school grades by observing their students during recess. Mary and Susy are the students Mrs. Jackson decides to observe the first day of school. Both join the line in front of the drinking fountain before going out to play. Mary quietly takes her place at the end of the line, where other schoolmates are grumbling about the length of the line. Susy tries to shove her way into the front of the line. One of her schoolmates tells Susy that Mrs. Jackson is watching, but Susy continues her efforts. Finally another schoolmate tells Susy that those who wait in line will be allowed to jump rope with the older girls. Susy immediately takes her place at the end of the line.

Mrs. Jackson from these observations decides that Mary is at Kohlberg's interpersonal concordance stage because of her consideration of her schoolmates, while Susy is at Kohlberg's instrumental relativist stage because of her reaction to rewards. Until completing her assessment of the rest of the students, Mrs. Jackson uses this knowledge in an informal way. She notices when Susy acts with consideration for her peers and rewards her with attention and praise. She notices when Mary obeys school rules both when approved by her peers, as at the drinking fountain, and when her peers are ignoring the rules, as when some of her schoolmates push to get out the door at lunchtime. She notices Mary's respect for rules whenever it is manifested and acknowledges this respect.

Junior High School

Junior high school students will be at Piaget's morality of cooperation stage because of their cognitive ability to view situations from another's point of view and their ability to objectively evaluate a situation. However, their being at Piaget's morality of cooperation stage does not presuppose the conventional level of Kohlberg's hierarchy because self-centeredness can exist without egocentricism or subjective realism. While most junior high school students should be at Kohlberg's conventional level, a slow rate of development or a fixation at one of the lower stages may have occurred. Therefore teachers can expect to find the first four stages of Kohlberg's hierarchy within their classes. Again, teachers should begin the moral education program by assessing the current stage of each of their students.

The teacher may begin in the junior high school grades with Kohlberg's ten hypothetical dilemmas. Fred, one of Miss Gray's brighter students, expressed moral reasoning at the law-and-order stage in most of these dilemmas. Since Fred was a quiet student who liked to read and work on his own, and because of his difference in moral development from the rest of his class, Miss Gray planned a literature program for Fred in conjunction with a language arts and history project. Among the books available for Fred to select were historical books concerning the American Revolution, the Civil War, and World War II, political documents concerning questionable presidential decisions and the riots of the 60s, and novels concerning possible utopias and characters faced with difficult moral decisions.

The IGE School

An IGE school employing a program for developing values which are consonant with moral development theories is Wilson Elementary School in Janesville, Wisconsin. Mary Baban, the leader of one of the primary units composed of students age 6 to 8, employs a film-strip series entitled *A Strategy for Teaching Values: Sound Filmstrips for the Primary Years* during the homeroom period. At this time, the students view one of the story dilemmas contained in the series and engage in a group discussion of what the characters should do and how the story will end.

Conclusion

These examples of the application of a moral education curriculum depict a number of different assessment methods and program possibilities. These methods and programs present ways of implementing a moral development curriculum using the Individually Guided Education programming model in the IGE school. Many other ways of implementing such a program exist. Through understanding the theories of Piaget and Kohlberg and their adaptability for stimulating moral development in an IGE school, teachers through IGE should be able to plan for the individual moral development needs of each of their students.

SUGGESTED READINGS FOR CHAPTER 6

Kohlberg, L., J. Rest, and E. Turiel 1969. Level of moral development as a determinant of preference and comprehension of moral judgments made by others. *Journal of Personality* 37: 225-252.

This article presents one research study Kohlberg cites to substantiate his hypothesis that moral development occurs in a fixed series of six stages. In this study, subjects were presented with answers to moral dilemmas that were at levels of moral reasoning above and below their own level. They were then questioned concerning their answer preference and their understanding of the reasoning involved in each answer.

Kohlberg, L., and E. Turiel 1971. Moral development and moral education. In G. S. Lesser (ed.), *Psychology and educational practice*. Glenview, Ill.: Scott Foresman, 1971.

This chapter discusses some of the educational implications of Kohlberg's theory and makes concrete suggestions as to how the teacher can foster moral development both through a planned program and through proper handling of student behavior problems.

Hoffman, M. L. 1970. Moral development. In P. Mussen (ed.), *Carmichael's manual of child psychology*. Vol. 2. (3rd ed.) New York: Wiley.

This chapter contains a summary of the moral development theories of Piaget, Kohlberg, and affective development theorists who have addressed the question of how an individual develops values. Thus this selection provides both a summary and a synthesis of the manner in which the area of moral development and the domain of affective development are related.

REFERENCES

Allen, D. W., and E. Seifman (eds.) 1971. *The teacher's handbook*. Glenview, Ill.: Scott Foresman.

Alston, W. P. 1971. Comments on Kohlberg's "From 'is' to 'ought'." In T. Mischel (ed.), *Cognitive development and epistemology*. New York: Academic Press.

Coleman, J. C. 1969. *Psychology and effective behavior*. Glenview, Ill.: Scott Foresman.

Communications Research Machines, Inc. 1971. *Developmental psychology today*. Del Mar, Calif.

Communications Research Machines, Inc. 1973. *Educational psychology: a contemporary view*. Del Mar, Calif.

Di Vesta, F. J., and G. G. Thompson 1970. *Educational psychology: instruction and behavioral change*. New York: Appleton-Century-Crofts.

Freud, S. 1938. *The basic writings of Sigmund Freud*. A. A. Brill (ed. and tr.) New York: Modern Library.

Garrison, K. C., and R. Magoon 1972. *Educational psychology: an integration of psychology and educational practices.* Columbus, Ohio: Merrill.

Garry, R., and H. L. Kingsley 1970. *The nature and conditions of learning.* (3rd ed.) Englewood Cliffs, N. J.: Prentice-Hall.

Hartshorne, H., and M. A. May 1928–30. *Studies in the nature of character.* Vol. 1: *Studies in deceit;* Vol. 2: *Studies in service and self-control;* Vol. 3: *Studies in the organization of character.* New York: Macmillan.

Hoffman, M. L. 1970. Moral development. In P. Mussen (ed.), *Carmichael's manual of child psychology.* Vol. 2. (3rd ed.) New York: Wiley.

Johnson, R. C. 1962. A study of children's moral judgments. *Child Development* 33: 327–354.

Kohlberg, L. 1971a. From "is" to "ought": how to commit the naturalistic fallacy and get away with it in the study of moral development. In T. Mischel (ed.), *Cognitive development and epistemology.* New York: Academic Press.

———— 1971b. Stages of moral development as a basis for moral education. In C. M. Beck, B. S. Crittenden, and E. Sullivan (eds.), *Moral education: interdisciplinary approaches.* Toronto: University of Toronto Press.

————, and E. Turiel 1971. Moral development and moral education. In G. S. Lesser (ed.), *Psychology and educational practice.* Glenview, Ill.: Scott Foresman.

———— 1970. Education for justice: a modern statement of the Platonic view. In N. F. Sizer and T. R. Sizer (eds.), *Moral education: five lectures.* Cambridge, Mass.: Harvard University Press.

———— 1969a. Development of children's orientations toward a moral order. In R. C. Sprinthall and N. A. Sprinthall (eds.), *Educational psychology: selected readings.* New York: Van Nostrand.

———— 1969b. Stage and sequence: the cognitive-developmental approach to socialization. In D. A. Goslin (ed.), *Handbook of socialization theory and research.* Chicago: Rand McNally.

————, J. Rest, and E. Turiel 1969. Level of moral development as a determinant of preference and comprehension of moral judgments made by others. *Journal of Personality* 37:225–252.

———— 1968. The child as a moral philosopher. *Psychology Today* 2(4): 25–30.

———— 1966. Moral education in the schools: a developmental view. *The School Review* 74: 1–30.

———— 1964. Development of moral character and moral ideology. In M. L. Hoffman and L. W. Hoffman (eds.), *Review of child development research.* New York: Russell Sage Foundation.

Longstreth, L. E. 1968. *Psychological development of the child.* New York: The Ronald Press.

MacRae, D., Jr. 1954. A test of Piaget's theories of moral development. *Journal of Abnormal and Social Psychology* 49: 14–18.

Mussen, P. H., J. J. Congor, and J. Kagan, 1969. *Child development and personality*. New York: Harper & Row.

Peters, R. S. 1971. Moral development: a plea for pluralism. In T. Mischel (ed.), *Cognitive development and epistemology*. New York: Academic Press.

Piaget, J. 1965. *The moral judgment of the child*. New York: Free Press.

Roblee, K. 1973. Kohlberg's theory of moral development and its application in educational institutions. Unpublished manuscript, Marquette University.

Sanborn, S. 1973. Means and ends: moral development and moral education. *Annual editions: readings in human development '73–'74*. Guilford, Conn.: Dushkin Publishing (*Harvard Graduate School of Education Bulletin*, Fall, 1971.)

Smart, M. S., and R. C. Smart 1972. *Children: development and relationships*. (2nd ed.) New York: Macmillan.

A strategy for teaching values: sound filmstrips for the primary years 1972. Pleasantville, N. Y.: Guidance Associates.

Toward moral maturity 1973. *Annual editions: readings in human development '73–'74*. Guilford, Conn.: Dushkin. (*Time Magazine*, June 28, 1971.)

Travers, J. 1970. *Fundamentals of educational psychology*. Scranton, Pa.: International Textbook.

Turiel, E. 1966. An experimental test of the sequentiality of developmental stages in the child's moral judgments. *Journal of Personality and Social Psychology* 3: 611–618.

Watson, R. and H. Lindgre 1973. *Psychology of the child*. New York: Wiley.

7

Physical and Psychomotor Development

Objectives

Upon completion of this chapter, the reader should be able:

- To comprehend the general topics which are critical to the growth process.
- To state the major periods of physical development, and recognize normal growth patterns.
- To note the relationship between advancement in psychomotor ability and maturation in physical growth for each major period of a student's physical development.
- To understand Harrow's *Taxonomy of the Psychomotor Domain* and how it can be applied in the classroom.
- To describe how the IGE school provides for psychomotor development.

> *Since the body is the pipe*
> *through which we tap all the succors*
> *and virtues of the material world,*
> *it is certain that a sound body*
> *must be at the root of any excellence*
> *in manners and actions.*
>
> Ralph Waldo Emerson

DEVELOPMENT IN THE PHYSICAL AND PSYCHOMOTOR DOMAINS AND THEIR EDUCATIONAL IMPLICATIONS

Observable movement behaviors are the outcome of psychomotor development. These behaviors extend from the simple reflexes evident at birth to the complex creative movements of an artist in the act of modifying raw media into a finished art object. Movement behaviors have physical and mental components and, as such, skilled psychomotor performance is influenced by both physical and perceptual development. Teachers seem to be more aware of certain individual differences in physical development than individual differences in perceptual development as it influences psychomotor performance. The reason for this awareness is quite apparent. Schools are filled with students whose physical appearances differ greatly. Differences in height, weight, shape, and so forth are readily apparent. But psychomotor development extends beyond these evident characteristics to perceptual and motor development as well. As a result, this chapter presents information about physical development as well as perceptual and motor development in an attempt to explain how the unique movement behaviors of children develop and how they can be nurtured by appropriate educational experiences.

PHYSICAL DEVELOPMENT AND ITS EDUCATIONAL IMPLICATIONS

The Growth Process

Physical growth processes do not occur in a haphazard manner. Within limited ranges, the rate of growth and the final size and structure of the human organism can be predicted (Tanner 1970). This prediction is possible because genes are programmed to regulate growth. By comparing the physical development of twins raised apart, researchers were initially able to observe the influence of genes upon the human growth process. Since then, the study of genetics has confirmed the influence of hereditary factors on human physical development. However, because of the influence of environmental factors such as nutrition, disease, physical trauma, and psychological stress, exact prediction of the rate of growth and the final size and structural characteristics of a person, from knowledge of that person's genetic background, is not possible. Researchers initially studied the influence of environment upon the human growth process through individuals suffering severe malnutrition, illness, or emotional trauma. Presently, they are giving more attention to the interaction of less abnormal environmental conditions and genetic factors, and they seem to favor the interactive position in the nature-nurture controversy. From these observations concerning physical development, teachers should realize that within a certain range, students' rate of growth and structural characteristics are set. Thus those students who are having difficulty adjusting to their personal physical characteristics such as height should be aided in their attempts to adjust rather than be given false hopes. Yet, teachers should not overlook the influence of environmental factors. For example, diet may be a primary contributing factor in student obesity, gauntness, or lethargy. When it is, teachers may provide dietary instruction or even provide special meals for students if it is possible and necessary.

Additional topics concerning the growth process and their educational implications which may be considered in studying human physical development are: (1) stages of physical development, (2) critical periods, (3) variations in the speed of development of structures and functions, and (4) the tendency to maintain a consistent growth curve and to accelerate growth when factors cause a temporary growth stoppage or slowdown.

For years developmental psychologists have discussed whether development is basically a continuous process or a more discrete system of stages. Most studies seem to indicate the importance of considering physical development as a continuous process. While there may be external indications that one suddenly develops at puberty, a closer look at this period of growth points to continuity in it. This does not imply that a stoppage or even temporary reversal of a developmental trend may not occur. It can and sometimes does. For example, a child's weight may remain constant or even temporarily decrease. However, over a period of time a pattern of continuous development emerges which teachers may utilize and take into account as they provide experiences for the individual students in their classes.

Critical periods are limited time spans during which a response is facilitated in an organism as a result of environmental "triggering" or as a result of other developments occurring within the organism. The detection of critical periods in humans is extremely difficult. While there is considerable evidence concerning the existence of critical periods in animals, evidence necessary to substantiate the idea that a human response must occur during certain periods, if it is ever to occur, does not exist. Rather, the limited research that has been conducted in this area suggests that there may be some sensitive periods in human development when a motor skill can be learned to a higher level of proficiency than if the skill is learned during a different period of development. For example, McGraw (1935) in a comparative study involving a set of twins found that early training in roller skating resulted in one twin being more proficient in this skill at a later age, while early training in tricycling did not have the same effect. Thus early practice seems to have a significant effect on some psychomotor activities but not on others. While only limited research has been conducted in this area of development, the teacher should be alert to the possibility that such sensitive periods may exist in the physical and motor development of students, and stay abreast of new, relevant research in this area.

One of the important factors related to individual differences is the rates of development of different body structures and different body functions, such as the secretion of certain hormones. Throughout physical development various body structures develop independently. However, it is generally the rule that the different structures develop at rates which allow normal development of psychomotor skills. For instance, toddlers develop the skeletal and muscular structure which enables them to walk, yet the amount of fatty tissue remaining in their bodies, the flexibility of their joints, and a lack of refined control over the smaller muscles of their bodies results in their walking with high steps and a waddle. Teachers should consider differences in developmental rates of body functions and structures when planning student activities. The cephalocaudal and proximodistal developmental patterns (Chapter 2) furnish useful guidelines. Perceptual recognition occurs before the ability to reproduce what one sees. For example, children are able to recognize a triangle before they are able to copy or draw a triangle. General control over the muscles of the hands and fingers is achieved before specific control. For example, children are able to satisfactorily draw straight lines, which require little muscular control, before they are able to satisfactorily draw curves and circles, which require a greater amount of muscular control.

Large muscle control is accomplished before the child gains control over smaller muscles.

Humans have the ability to return to an original growth curve after having been deterred from their normal growth curve by various environmental factors such as illness or malnutrition. Waddington (1957) refers to this ability as homeorhesis. When homeorhesis occurs, the organism's growth rate accelerates for a period of time to compensate for the time in which physical growth was hindered. When the environmental hindrance to growth was mild and of short duration, homeorhesis allows the organism to gain the growth that should have occurred previously and returns the organism to its normal growth pattern. However, when illness, malnutrition, and other like factors are severe and persist for long periods of time, the process of homeorhesis does not totally regain the physical growth that should have occurred. Since more physical energy is involved in an accelerated growth rate than is normally expended, students who have been ill are less active than usual upon first returning to school. They also may have fallen behind their schoolmates in physical growth and/or psychomotor development if the illness lasted more than a few days. Teachers should avoid becoming unduly concerned, for the process of homeorhesis will return students to their normal performance level provided they have the opportunity to acquire the academic skills they missed during their absence.

NORMAL PHYSICAL DEVELOPMENTAL PATTERNS DURING THE SCHOOL YEARS

This section, which is based largely on Bucher (1956) and Kirchner (1956), will concentrate upon the periods of physical development from approximately age five to maturity, for it is during this time that the teacher is in contact with the maturing child. Thus the subsequent paragraphs will consider development during the primary school years, the intermediate school years, and the high school years.

The Primary School Years

During the primary school years (age five to eight) students are in the physical development period described as childhood. The skeletal development of primary school students is characterized by a softness or sponginess of the bones in the extremities. Deformity of bone structure can easily occur during this time since bones may split or break without protruding through the skin's surface. The likelihood of such occurrences is magnified by the increase in student proneness to accidents because of their newly mastered motor skills and their adventuresome spirit. Teachers may be required at times to place restrictions on the types of activities these students choose.

Muscular development in students of this age is characterized by a gradual loss of baby fat and a gradual increase in muscular tissue. This results in an increase in physical strength, especially in the arms and legs. The child's physical potential in the area of strength can be fostered at this time by vigorous, large-muscle activities such as chasing, climbing, and jumping. Often the students' need for vigorous activity during this period is discharged in the classroom where they will alternate between sitting and standing, or even "roughhousing" when they are supposed to be engaged in activities restricting the use of the larger muscles. Frequent breaks for recess or exercise are necessary for primary school children. However, at these times, because the students' muscles are in a state of development, they are susceptible to sudden fatigue which they may not wish to acknowledge. At times, teachers may need to restrain the desire to continue strenuous activity in children suffering from fatigue. Rapid recovery from fatigue occurs when the healthy student rests.

While growth is proceeding in all muscular tissue during this period, the large muscles of the arms and legs are more fully developed than the small muscles of the hands and fingers. Consequently, activities requiring the use of these small muscles require greater effort for these students than for older students. However, such activities are necessary for the development of the hand and finger muscles, as well as for the development of eye-hand coordination. Special motor instruments such as thick pencils are often recommended to aid the transition of muscular skills in developing students of this age.

A slowness in reaction time when compared to adults is also a characteristic of primary school students. While the time these children require to respond is gradually shortening, teachers will observe a difference between their own reaction time and that of these students. Therefore, patience is necessary when dealing with children of this age.

The development of organs in the primary school student is characterized by (1) a small but rapidly growing heart and (2) lungs which are proportionately smaller than other organs because they have developed at a slower rate. The size of primary school children's heart and lungs is a factor in their susceptibility to fatigue and rapid recovery after rest. In addition, their hearts can easily be strained or damaged by the contagious diseases of childhood which rapidly spread from student to student during this initial time of close contact with many other people. The relative size of the lungs in proportion with the rest of the body increases the vulnerability of these students to respiratory diseases and infections such as colds and tonsillitis. Primary school teachers, as contrasted to teachers of older children, can expect a greater amount of student absence due to illness. They also must be more aware of physical symptoms of illness to avoid the spreading of contagious disease among their students.

Another organ which has not fully developed in the primary school student is the eye. Until approximately the age of eight, the eyeballs of most students are shallow or flat, rather than round. This results in an inability to clearly focus upon small, near-point objects, difficulty in judging spatial relationships, and a tendency toward eye fatigue and irritation. Until the eye has matured, reading materials should be printed in large letters, writing paper should have large spaces, and activities involving near-point vision should be short and interspersed with activities which do not require close visual attention to small detail.

The Intermediate School Years

During the intermediate school years (ages eight to twelve) students move from the physical development period described by developmentalists as childhood to that described as adolescence. The skeletal growth of younger intermediate school students (ages eight to ten) proceeds gradually, with a small lag prior to the beginning of pubescence. During this period females are about a year ahead of males in skeletal maturity. However, both males and females demonstrate vast individual differences in the hardness of their bones. Consequently, bone fractures may still be visually undetectable. Students are still accident prone during this time, and teachers may have to place restrictions on their daredevil activities.

The skeletal development of older intermediate school students (age ten to twelve) is in a transitional period. At this time a growth spurt signifying the onset of pubescence occurs in most females and some males. By approximately the age of eleven, girls are usually taller and heavier than boys. Poor coordination may appear in those students whose rate of skeletal development and muscular development is disproportionate. Other physically based traits which may be displayed by students at this time are plumpness, slow movement, apathy, poor posture, fatigue, irritability, fluctuations in alertness, and/or embarrassment about physiological differences. Teachers should apply common sense when dealing with such problems, realizing that most will disappear, but some, such as poor posture or embarrassment, may require intervention on their part.

The muscular development of the younger intermediate school student is manifested in continual development of manipulative skills and eye-hand coordination due to the maturing of small muscles. Poor posture at this age is often due to the unequal rate of development of the small muscles in comparison to that of skeletal development. Body control, strength, and endurance should be stressed at this time through classroom activities and physical activities requiring the use of the entire body.

The muscular development of older intermediate school students proceeds at a rapid rate. In males a greater gain in muscular strength is exhibited at this time than in females. A decrease in muscular flexibility is also manifested at this time, which appears to be due to the types of activities students engage in, rather than physiological reasons. Males display a greater loss in muscular flexibility than females. At this age underdeveloped or unskilled students may be self-conscious about engaging in new activities, or activities in which they perform poorly. Teachers should encourage the participation of such students because exercise is necessary to maximize inherited potential. Movements requiring flexibility should be stressed to reduce the loss of the muscles' ability to stretch.

The organic development of younger intermediate school students is characterized by a heart which is developing at a slower rate than the body, glandular changes preparatory to the onset of pubescence, and maturation of the eye. Damage to the heart is less probable at this time than at a younger age because the skeletal muscles fatigue first and the student has become immune to many of the contagious diseases of childhood. Modesty in physical appearance first manifests itself around this time, as does difficulty seeing distant objects (myopia, or nearsightedness). Teachers should recognize that eyeglasses correct some, but not all, visual problems and should arrange their classes so that students with visual or hearing defects are in a favorable location.

The organic development of older intermediate school students is characterized by (1) a heart which still is growing at a slower rate than other body parts and (2) the onset of puberty. The size of the heart in relation to the rest of the body may cause a decrease in blood pressure. Fatigue may occur in students who are active for long periods of time or who participate in too many activities. The possibility of fatigue increases at this time because students are competitive and tend to push themselves, some even going beyond the point of fatigue. Chronic tension and irritability are the result of a constant state of fatigue. Puberty with its accompanying physiological changes begins to occur at this time with the development of the breasts and pubic hair preceding the onset of menstruation in females, and the development of pubic hair and genital growth preceding the development of facial hair and the first seminal ejaculation in males. The change of voice pitch is one of the more noticeable results of puberty in males. Differentiation of physical activities and requirements for males and females is recommended at this time because of the sexual differences which are beginning to exist.

The High School Years

During the high school years (age twelve to eighteen) most students complete the physical development period called adolescence. The skeletal development of junior high school students is characterized by an increase in bone length and width. Girls are approximately two years ahead of boys in physical and sexual development at this time and consequently are more interested in boys than boys in their age group are in girls. Some females will attain their adult height by the end of junior high school while others will continue to grow beyond that point. Males, being slower in skeletal development, continue to grow well into the high school years and sometimes into their twenties. Skeletal growth stops when sexual development is completed.

During the high school years, the facial and body contours of the adult are attained, and sexual differences between males and females become more pronounced and apparent. The pelvis of the female is broader proportionately than that of the male, and often will continue to broaden into the twenties. Activities which result in pull or pressure to this area of the female's body should be avoided. Because of this difference in pelvic structure, the legs of the female join the pelvis at an angle, resulting in a difference in how the female walks and runs. The shoulders of the male are proportionately broader than those of the female, and the male's shoulder and arm muscles are stronger. Males are thus able to support more weight in this area of their body than are females. These differences also result in a difference between the sexes as to the body's center of gravity which is lower in females.

The muscular development of students is nearing completion by the end of junior high school with a corresponding increase in coordination. The muscles of the male are becoming hard and firm, while those of the female remain soft. A marked difference in strength in favor of the male is evident. Differences in the physical activities required of males and females are now essential. Because of the development of the muscles and muscular control, posture is improving, and grace and coordination are evident in the students' movements.

The development of the organs during this time is most evident in the rapid development of the sexual organs with corresponding physical and psychological implications. Teachers should aid students in coping with their new physical and psychological desires.

During the junior high school years, the heart is increasing in size at a rapid rate which may be out of proportion to the rate of development of the arteries. Overexertion should be avoided at this time to prevent damage to the arteries. Glandular instability is also quite prevalent in the high school years, resulting in fluctuations in energy level, headaches, nosebleeds, nervousness, heart palpitations, and skin blemishes. Students should be assured that these physical problems are usually just temporary although medical consultation is recommended.

TAXONOMY OF THE PSYCHOMOTOR DOMAIN

In order to relate the psychomotor domain to physical development and other aspects of the learning process, it is necessary to have a thorough system which orders and organizes psychomotor behaviors. Harrow (1972) recognized the need for such a system and classified the types of psychomotor behavior in a hierarchical arrangement. Figure 7.1 illustrates this hierarchical order as articulated in Harrow's *Taxonomy of the Psychomotor Domain*. In this book the broad categories and subcategories of psychomotor behavior are examined in a

6.00	Nondiscursive communication
5.00	Skilled movements
4.00	Physical abilities
3.00	Perceptual abilities
2.00	Basic-fundamental movements
1.00	Reflex movements

Fig. 7.1 The major classifications in Harrow's *Taxonomy of the Psychomotor Domain* (1972).

developmental context and examples of objectives for each subcategory are given.

The first category, reflex movements, includes involuntary movements which are responses to stimuli without conscious volition. Harrow pointed out that this classification level does not lend itself to behavioral objectives and that it was included in the taxonomy only because it is the foundation upon which learners build their movement repertoires.

The basic-fundamental movements which make up the second level of the taxonomy are observed in the first year of infancy. The movements in this classification are based on the reflex movements which are part of the first classification level. Activities in this level include such behavior as the infant's grasping and the sequential activities leading to walking behavior which emerge without training.

While the third classification, perceptual abilities, may seem more cognitive than psychomotor, it is included in the psychomotor taxonomy because of its inseparability from motor functions. This classification includes kinesthetic, visual, auditory, and tactile discriminations as well as eye-hand and eye-foot coordination. The improvement of perceptual abilities depends upon maturation and learning, and the sharpening of perceptual abilities is a necessary step in the improvement of motor behavior. This classification level has special significance for educators who are concerned with remediation of learning difficulties because it lists the prerequisite skills specialists (Frostig, Maslow, Lefever, and Whittlesey 1963; Roach and Kephart 1966) have found to be necessary for mastery of primary school skills.

The fourth classification, physical abilities, considers the physical abilities which are necessary for motor performance including endurance, strength, flexibility, agility, reaction-response time, and dexterity. Thus this class spells out those physical characteristics which can be limiting or facilitating factors in the successful performance of skilled movements, the fifth classification.

Skilled movements make up the fifth classification in Harrow's taxonomy. Since skill implies a degree of efficiency in performing an activity, Harrow included in this level those movement behaviors which include both learning and a considerable degree of complexity. This latter requirement is necessary to separate the category from the second classication level. Skilled movements require both learning and practice for their successful execution.

Finally, the sixth classification, nondiscursive communication, includes both innate and learned behaviors. Examples of innate-movement communications are crying responses and fear responses. An example of a learned-movement communication would be waving to someone.

Harrow's taxonomy of psychomotor behavior can be a useful tool in helping teachers devise programs and establish goals in the psychomotor area. Just as it is crucial to classify student learning experiences and define objectives in proper sequence for behaviors in the cognitive and affective domains, it is also important for this to be done in the psychomotor domain. Throughout the taxonomy the importance of both perceptual and motor development is implied. It is in the school setting where these processes are necessary prerequisites for success in curricular areas, and the taxonomy identifies both classifications and sequences for teachers and curriculum developers.

PSYCHOMOTOR DEVELOPMENT AND THE INDIVIDUALLY GUIDED EDUCATION SCHOOL CURRICULUM

Introduction

Psychomotor development influences student performance and student achievement in all curricular areas. However, a higher level of psychomotor development is required for the achievement of success by students in some curricular areas than in others. Educators generally consider reading, spelling, mathematics, and so forth, as curricular areas requiring a minimum of psychomotor development. In contrast, curricular areas such as physical education, handwriting, art, and music are regarded by educators as requiring a greater amount of psychomotor development. Consequently, this portion of the chapter will consider separately the psychomotor development necessary for student success in school generally and the psychomotor development necessary for student success in specific curricular areas.

Psychomotor Abilities and Success in School

Maturational factors which are prerequisites for the development of psychomotor abilities, such as the ability of the eye to focus clearly upon letters, numbers, and small objects, are important for success in most school activities. Until approximately the age of eight, the physical structure of the eye in most students has not fully developed, and such students will have difficulty focusing on small print or objects. Consequently, large print and objects should be used by teachers during the primary school years and afterward when such an individual difference in psychomotor development is apparent. Also, during the primary school years, the eye muscles are susceptible to fatigue, and school tasks involving long periods of close visual work should be discouraged.

Experiential factors such as prior practice in eye-hand coordination may also play an important role in the achievement of success in school. While the development of eye-hand coordination is influenced by maturation, the effects of practice should not be underestimated. Most psychomotor skills are subject to marked improvement as a result of practice. The student who has had more prior practice in activities requiring eye-hand coordination will probably be better able to perform school skills requiring this psychomotor ability, just as most people are able to write more legibly using one hand rather than the other even though the structure of both physical appendages is nearly the same.

Teachers who are aware of student differences in physical maturation and practice of psychomotor movements can utilize this knowledge to plan academic programs suitable to each student. When the psychomotor behavior of the student suggests a delay in physical maturation, the teacher can devise instructional programs which foster cognitive development but are not dependent on physical capabilities the student does not presently possess. When the psychomotor behavior of certain students suggests practice will increase their psychomotor performance, provisions for such practice can be furnished in the instructional program. For example, at Parkview School, an IGE school in Cedarburg, Wisconsin, a psychomotor development center is part of the Instructional Materials Center (IMC). Students may utilize this center through their own volition, or teachers may prescribe the use of a part or all of the center for particular children. While the content of the center changes throughout the school year, it concentrates on the development of small-muscle coordination, sensory discrimination, and auditory-perception skills. Some exemplary materials included in this center are jigsaw puzzles; mazes; and colored pegs, pegboards, and design cards.

The IGE school allows for lags in the psychomotor development of some children and also for extraordinary growth spurts in others. The nature of the individualization in teaching allows for a high degree of sensitivity in detecting psychomotor factors affecting students and for the fostering of psychomotor abilities in the desired directions.

IGE can be maximally effective in the learning process in relation to physical growth and psychomotor development. However, there is a requirement which is necessary before the IGE school can be effective in the psychomotor domain. This obvious requirement is that the teachers must have a thorough knowledge of physical growth and psychomotor development. Furthermore, teachers must understand how physical growth and psychomotor development relate to the intellectual and affective domains.

Because the IGE school recognizes that no two students are exactly alike in their development and ability levels, it establishes instructional strategies to optimize individual student learning. This individualization certainly is necessary in the more cognitive type of school learning, but also in the psychomotor areas.

Physical Education

Physical education is one of the readily recognized areas in which physical and psychomotor development play an essential role in student performance and student achievement of success. Since physical education is principally concerned with gross motor learning involving neuromuscular activity, individual differences in the maturation of both the nervous system and the muscular system, as well as differences in prior learning experiences, are reflected in the child's psychomotor performance. Consequently, an effective physical education curriculum must take into account individual differences in maturation and prior learning. Such a curriculum can be feasibly organized in IGE schools.

Proponents of traditional physical education for the most part have ignored individual differences in planning their curricula and establishing objectives. In the traditional physical education class all students, no matter what their level of ability may be, learn to participate in team sports and structured exercise sessions. The classroom, or gym, is a competitive environment in which many students are unable to meet the expected standards. Often this causes students to lose interest in physical education and may instill feelings of inferiority in them when their performance is far below that of their peers.

A new trend in elementary physical education known as move-

Each student solves problems according to the individual's psychomotor abilities.

ment education offers many possibilities for the IGE school and solutions to the problems of traditional physical education. Although movement education is relatively new to the United States, it has been used in England's elementary schools since World War II. Movement education offers both a philosophy and a teaching approach for physical education.

The goal of movement education is to help students learn basic movement patterns and coordinate these movement patterns into purposive action. Bucher (1968) defines movement education as:

> ... individual exploration of the ability of the body to relate and react to the physical concepts of the environment, and to factors in the environment, be they material or human.

There is no competition in movement education. All students are given a problem such as moving through some kind of obstacle course in a confined space, and are free to solve it in their own way. In movement education there is no one right way to solve a problem of movement. All students must discover the solution which best fits their own needs and abilities. Students work at a solution to the problem at their own speed. Once the problem is solved, a slightly more difficult problem is tackled.

The role of teachers in movement education differs from the teacher's role in traditional physical education. Movement education teachers assist the students in solving problems and may offer suggestions, but they never instruct students in the solving of a problem or demonstrate how the problem should be solved. It is up to the children to solve the problem encountered in movement education in their own unique way.

Although the student is given freedom in problem solving, the program is based on an organized, structured set of objectives and activities to meet these objectives. In the early elementary school years, activities which will promote the development of gross motor abilities are carried on. As individual children master these movements, they move on to progressively more difficult tasks which require a refinement of motor movements. All children begin the program at their own level of ability and progress at their own rate of speed. In this way, children are not forced to compete with their peers and experience repeated failures.

The movement education approach to physical education removes the competitive environment of traditional physical education programs and allows every student to experience success. Its goal is not to teach students the specific psychomotor skills of individual and team sports, but rather it assists all students in developing an awareness of the basic movement patterns of their bodies and the ways in which their bodies can act upon and react to stimuli in their environment. In this way it teaches movement patterns which are useful throughout life rather than specific skills which may be used by most people during their school years only. Also, by concentrating on activities which develop gross motor movements in the elementary school years, it gives students the necessary foundation for learning finer motor movements as they mature. Movement education is an approach to physical education which recognizes individual differences and attempts to meet the needs of each student, which is the aim of the IGE program.

Handwriting

It is often observed that students with poor handwriting skills perform below that level which would be expected of them on the basis of their intellectual ability. While these students might know the answers, their poor development in handwriting skills does not provide them with the ability to translate their thoughts into written words. As a result of their inability to write legibly or to perform written tasks, they become frustrated and eventually might refuse to begin lessons, thinking that not finishing in time often results in punishment from the teacher anyway. At this point the learning process has broken down. Clearly what students of this type need is an individualized program providing them with the necessary elements to meet with personal successes and, ultimately, to meet with performance levels which are expected at their age.

In the IGE school, it would be quite unlikely to observe a stoppage in the learning process because a student lacked handwriting skills. It is not being implied here that all students in an IGE school are excellent in handwriting skills. Rather, it is recognized that students have different handwriting abilities, and just because some students are experiencing difficult times in their fine motor coordination, this will not stop the learning process. These students would be required to demonstrate their handwriting skills only in ways in which they could experience success. Their instructional program might emphasize general movements which would be designed to improve their coordination and eventually their handwriting skills.

A study investigating the various methods of handwriting instruction at the third and fourth grade levels at Giese Elementary School in Racine, Wisconsin, resulted in important implications for the teaching of handwriting in the IGE school (Tagatz, Otto, Klausmeier, Goodwin, and Cook 1968). Three main approaches to the teaching of handwriting were studied. The traditional approach, or the formal group approach, was based on a program of study developed by a commercial publisher and involved teaching handwriting to an entire group of students. The formal-individualized method of instruction likewise followed the instructional program of a commercial organization, but allowed students to work at their own pace and to concentrate on their individual problems within the limits set by the commercial materials. The third method of handwriting instruction was the individualized-diagnostic approach. With this method, students were given individual assistance with their particular problems, but were not given commercial materials to use. Students were urged to continuously evaluate their own handwriting, especially in respect to the specific difficulties they experienced.

One of the principal findings of the study was that the traditional formal group approach to handwriting instruction was not as effective as the individualized-diagnostic approach. More significant differences among the methods employed were found on the third grade level than on the fourth grade level. The study indicated that the best approach to handwriting instruction for third grade pupils was the individualized-diagnostic method. Two factors may account for the lack of significant differences among methods in grade four. First, skills used in handwriting improve between the last half of grade three and the last half of grade four thus minimizing differences. Fourth graders have also received an additional year of instruction in one method and have already formed certain writing habits on the basis of this instruction.

Several important implications for handwriting instruction were drawn from the results of this study. It was suggested by the researchers (Tagatz et al. 1968) that: "Perhaps the critical factor in the early development of legible handwriting is individualized attention, yet this same individualization may not be nearly so effective after pupils' handwriting habits have been fairly well established." They further suggested on the basis of this investigation that the most effective procedure for teaching handwriting at the third grade level would be a combination of the individualized-diagnostic approach and the formal-individualized approach. They urge that, if this combined approach is implemented, the curriculum should be modified in grades one through three, rather than following the suggestion of some commercial groups which claim the curriculum should be modified in the middle elementary grades. By the time children reach the middle grades, their handwriting habits have already been fairly well established and may be resistant to change. The setting of the IGE school is ideal for the type of approach to handwriting instruction proposed in this study.

Art

Art, as it is traditionally taught, frequently functions as a time filler when students finish assignments early, or as a reward for performing well in other subjects. Students are often asked to draw various objects and are evaluated on how well their drawing imitates the "real thing." Teachers base their judgments of students' art on adult tastes and values which young children cannot understand. Little attention is paid to children's individual interests and creativity. In planning art lessons, teachers often do not take into consideration differences in the physical and perceptual development of the students and try to evaluate the work of all students on the same basis.

Specialists in art education believe that there are stages in a child's art development which parallel the stages in physical and psychomotor development. These educators maintain that in order to understand and fully appreciate children's art, a teacher must be aware of how the stages in physical and psychomotor development are expressed in their art. Lowenfeld and Brittain (1970) cite five stages of the art development in the young child. These stages are referred to as (1) scribbling stage (2 to 4 years); (2) preschematic stage (4 to 7 years); (3) schematic stage (7 to 9 years); (4) dawning realism stage (9 to 11 years); and (5) pseudo-naturalism stage (11 to 13 years). In the scribbling stage, children take pleasure in making random marks on their paper. As they reach the age of four, the random marks become more organized and are more controlled. During the preschematic stage, young children attempt to represent objects in their environment. Their representations are frequently placed indiscriminately on the paper and differ very much in size. At this age, the children's drawings contain many head-feet representations of the human being. By the age of seven, or the schematic stage, children's drawings begin to symbolize various aspects of their environment. Children develop a concept of form and tend to arrange their objects horizontally at the bottom of the page. Children's drawings continually show less representation and more symbolism as they enter the stage of dawning realism. Because of growing self-awareness, their drawings of humans become more refined and detailed. During the pseudo-naturalistic stage, drawings of human figures are still more detailed and receive more emphasis on sexual differences. It is at this stage that the students begin to develop the concepts of depth, perspective, and color.

Recent studies have indicated that teaching has little or no effect on these stages until the child is about twelve years old and is able to portray concepts such as depth and perspective. Research indicates that all children must progress through each of these stages in art which are interrelated with physical and psychomotor development.

The rate with which children proceed from one stage to another may be speeded up to some degree when the opportunities and materials for drawing are made available to them. A study conducted by Salome (1965) supports the view that teaching has little or no effect on young children's art development. He found that training did not improve the art of fourth graders, but helped to a small degree to improve the work of fifth graders. Neperud (1966), however, conducted a study using fifth graders and found no significant improvement in art work as a result of training except with girls of high intelligence. It appears, therefore, that the teaching of skills and concepts in art has no significant effect on a children's art until they reach a certain stage in their development in which they possess the necessary psychomotor and cognitive abilities. Lowenfeld and Brittain (1970) conclude that:

> The teaching of art must start with the youngster and not be involved with externals. Changing or altering his drawing or painting to satisfy some whim of the art teacher will, in most cases, be incomprehensible to a child; it is the youngster himself and his interrelationship with his environment that becomes crucial.

Because of a growing concern for accountability in education, an art program must have a definite set of objectives and not merely serve as an added feature to the core subjects. Several objectives which should be included in those of a sound art program are (1) development of physical and psychomotor skills, (2) development of an aesthetic awareness, and (3) promotion of creative thinking.

The art experience can help young children relate their visual perceptions to their cognitive process. Through art young children become aware of various forms, dimensions of space, and colors in their environment and are able to impose some order upon all of these stimuli so that the stimuli become meaningful for them. In *Art education: elementary* (1972), the National Art Education Association suggests the ways in which an art program can promote the development of the child:

> The child who is trained to use his eyes from birth and to be aware of the formal elements of design, who can make visual analogies, infer relationships, and verbalize what is seen and understood, is most certainly better able to perceive visually than the child who is not given this training. He will also be more receptive to unfamiliar stimuli, less fearful of it, and more open to veridical perception after having been exposed to this training. Art educators must realize that the goals and content of this training lie to a great extent in their domain.

A second objective of art programs should be to promote an aesthetic awareness. Through art young children are exposed to many different shapes, sizes, and dimensions of space in the world around them and they can come to appreciate the beauty in these. Aesthetics cannot be taught in an academic fashion by merely teaching concepts such as color and perspective. Instead, the teacher must make certain experiences available to young children which will contribute to an aesthetic sense. Thus, students should be allowed freedom in their art work since an aesthetic experience is unique to the individual.

A third objective which should be included in a school art program is the promotion of creative thinking (Hoffa 1964). Art is a visual language which enables young children to express in their own individual ways how they perceive the world around them. With each art project, children should be challenged by the problem of finding

Art programs should promote psychomotor development, aesthetic awareness, and creative thinking.

their own solutions to putting various shapes, colors, ideas and feelings together in a meaningful work of art. Children should not be instructed to solve such a problem in a certain prescribed manner, but should be left to their own creative thinking. This kind of training in creative thinking will prepare children to deal with problems met in a society which is moving more and more into the realm of what is unknown.

The IGE school allows for individual differences in the physical and psychomotor development of children. Children are able to work at their own level and rate of speed. Consequently, the art program in the IGE curriculum recognizes that children differ from one another in their level of art development due to the differences in physical and psychomotor development. Children are not restricted in their drawings to the whims of a teacher, but are allowed to freely express themselves and the way they experience reality. In the IGE school, the art program is not seen as merely being a "dessert" after the "meat and potatoes" of reading, writing, and arithmetic. Instead, it serves the threefold purpose of promoting physical and psychomotor development, enhancing an aesthetic awareness, and promoting creative thinking.

Music

Traditionally, school music programs have been isolated from the rest of the curriculum and have been designed without any specific objectives besides the vague one of "teaching music to children" (Myers 1961). In the traditional school, music is often restricted to a certain hour in the day devoted just to music and is not integrated with any of the other subjects. The music program is geared to teaching certain concepts and skills at each grade level, regardless of the individual skills, needs, and previous experiences in music of students. Frequently, students who excel in musical talent are encouraged in their efforts, whereas the supposedly less talented student is given little help in improving weak areas such as rhythmic sense. In the traditional school, little attention is paid to the individual differences of students in their physical and psychomotor development and how they are related to a student's musical development.

In the IGE school, music is integrated with the rest of the curriculum in order to contribute to the process of learning by providing an opportunity for children to learn through activity rather than just discussion. For instance, mathematical concepts can be taught through music as is done on the popular television show "Sesame Street." Not only can the music program contribute to other areas of learning but it can also affect the physical and psychomotor development of children. Muscular coordination, for example, can be improved through rhythmic activities done to music.

The music program in the IGE school is designed to fit children rather than having children fit the program. All children are first assessed to determine their stage of physical and psychomotor development, their previous experiences in music, and the areas of weakness they may have as well as their particular strengths and interests. A

Muscular coordination can be improved through rhythmic activities.

music program which does not consider the differences among students may not greatly contribute to their learning and development and, in fact, could be detrimental to it. In a study of adolescent boys, Swanson (1959) found that many teachers did not consider differences in the stages of physical development between adolescent boys and girls when they designed their music programs. Many songs that were taught could be handled by the girls, but not by the boys who were experiencing a change in their voices. Consequently, the boys generally did less well than the girls and soon lost interest in the class. Swanson also suggests that such experiences could be harmful to the proper vocal development of the adolescent boys.

In the IGE school a music program can be developed which will be geared for each individual's stage in physical and psychomotor development in order to enhance further development. Rhythmic games and activities are engaged in which help to improve gross motor and fine motor skills that must be learned. Myers (1961) defines rhythms as "the combination of music and bodily movement in pattern." Activities such as clapping, skipping, and stepping to music can help to develop a sense of rhythm and improve muscular coordination. Children can start with rhythmic exercises which are appropriate for their stage of physical and psychomotor development and proceed at their own pace. As they become more advanced, various dance steps which require more muscular coordination and more difficult gross and fine motor skills can be introduced.

SUGGESTED READINGS FOR CHAPTER 7

Corner, G. W. 1944. *Ourselves unborn: an embryologist's essay on man.* New Haven: Yale University Press.

The author, assuming no previous knowledge of biology on the part of the reader, presents a brief description of human development in a manner intended to increase the reader's awareness of the importance of the growth process in education.

Harrow, A. 1972. *A taxonomy of the psychomotor domain.* New York: McKay.

The author provides for the reader a hierarchically arranged and developmentally sequenced behavioral taxonomy for the psychomotor domain. It is intended that a working knowledge of the behaviors identified and classified in the taxonomy will serve as a guide for those educators concerned with preparing meaningful sequential curriculum, applying appropriate instructional strategies, and selecting relevant measurement techniques for their students.

Lowenfeld, V., and W. Brittain 1970. *Creative and mental growth.* (5th ed.) New York: Macmillan.

The authors attempt to show that art is entwined with a child's creative and mental growth. It is their conviction that mental growth is not the development of intellectual capacity alone, rather it includes the acquisition of many interpersonal skills and intrapersonal qualities, many of which can be creatively developed and expressed in art. The book parallels for the reader a developmental sequence of psychological growth and creative skills which, along with suggestions for teaching methods in art, developing art programs and understanding the psychology of art, is intended to assist the educator in meeting the student's creative and mental growth needs.

REFERENCES

Bucher, C. A. 1956. *Foundations of physical education.* (2nd ed.) St. Louis: Mosby.

———— 1968. *Foundations of physical education.* (5th ed.) St. Louis: Mosby.

Corner, G. W. 1944. *Ourselves unborn: an embryologist's essay on man.* New Haven: Yale University.

Emerson, R. W. 1883. *Aristocracy: lectures and biographical sketches.* Vol. 10. Boston: Houghton-Mifflin.

Frostig, M., P. Maslow, D. W. Lefever, and J. R. Whittlesey 1963. *The Marianne Frostig developmental test of visual perception.* Palo Alto, Calif.: Consulting Psychologists. *Perceptual and Motor Skills* 19: 463–499.

Harrow, A. 1972. *A taxonomy of the psychomotor domain.* New York: McKay.

Hoffa, H. E. 1964. The relationship of art experience to conformity. In W. L. Brittain (ed.), *Creativity and art education.* Washington, D.C.: The National Art Education Association.

Kirchner, G. 1956. *Physical education for elementary school children.* (2nd ed.) St. Louis: Mosby.

Lowenfeld, V., and W. Brittain 1970. *Creative and mental growth.* (5th ed.) New York: Macmillan.

McGraw, M. B. 1935. *Growth: a study of Johnny and Jimmy.* New York: Appleton-Century.

Myers, L. 1961. *Teaching children music in the elementary school.* (3rd ed.) Englewood Cliffs, N. J.: Prentice-Hall.

National Art Education Association 1972. P. Greenberg (ed.), *Art education: elementary.* Washington, D.C.

Neperud, W. 1966. An experimental study of visual elements, selected art instruction methods, and drawing development at the fifth grade level. *Studies in Art Education* 7, 2.

Roach, E. G., and N. C. Kephart 1966. *The Purdue perceptual-motor survey.* Columbus, Ohio: Merrill.

Salome, R. A. 1965. The effects of perceptual training upon the two-dimensional drawings of children. *Studies in Art Education* 7, 1.

Swanson, F. J. 1959. Voice mutation in the adolescent male: an experiment in guiding the voice development of adolescent boys in general music classes. Unpublished doctoral dissertation. Madison, Wisc.: University of Wisconsin.

Tagatz, G. E., W. Otto, H. J. Klausmeier, W. L. Goodwin, and D. M. Cook 1968. Effect of three methods of instruction upon the handwriting performance of third and fourth graders. *American Educational Research Journal* 5, 1: 81–89.

Tanner, J. M. 1970. Physical growth. In P. H. Mussen (ed.), *Carmichael's manual of child psychology.* (3rd ed.) New York: Wiley.

Waddington, C. H. 1957. *The strategy of the genes: a discussion of some aspects of theoretical biology.* London: Allen & Unwin.

8

Epilogue: The Potential of Humankind

Objectives

Upon completion of this chapter, the reader should be able:

- To comprehend a three-dimensional model of human development and understand how it depicts humankind's initial, present, and potential states.
- To identify areas in which humankind's present understanding of development is incomplete.
- To recognize the need for a theory which incorporates the various viewpoints expressed in contemporary developmental theories.

---

*Much in you is still man
and much in you is not yet man
But a shapeless pigmy that
walks asleep in the mist
searching for its own awakening.*

Kahlil Gibran*

HUMAN DEVELOPMENTAL POTENTIAL

All individuals living in the world today are engaged in a growth process, their own unique becoming. The human species is also in the midst of growth, of becoming. The unknown future of humanity and of each individual looms on the horizon. What does the future hold for you? What will the future hold for your progeny? What is the future of the human race?

Each step in the sequence of evolution has brought people closer to realizing the human potential. In order for the successive generation to make the next evolutionary step it is necessary for an educational system to exist which first brings children to the level of the present generation. This fact has long been realized by many societies and cultures, but only recently has our society recognized that people may in fact be instrumental in their own evolutionary progression. As dynamic and interactive organisms, human beings are not only acted upon but also act upon other humans and/or things about them. As active organisms, humans participate in determining the future of their species. Education then, has two major purposes, the first being to transmit the cultural heritage of the past to successive generations, the second being to motivate individuals to creatively change, to transform, to make new, to make different, to improve.

In Chapter 2 it was stated that for purposes of study, psychologists and others break the human organism into constituent parts. This book has presented ideas about children in terms of their cognitive development, language development, affective development, moral development, and physical or psychomotor development. However, humans are not pieced-together creations, and human nature cannot be explained by merely adding human components together. Humans are more than the sum of their parts. Each individual is a dynamic

---

* Reprinted from *The prophet,* by Kahlil Gibran, with the permission of the publisher, Alfred A. Knopf, Inc. Copyright 1923 by Kahlil Gibran; renewal copyright 1951 by Administrators C.T.A. of Kahlil Gibran Estate, and Mary G. Gibran.

organism in which the constituent parts interact with one another, with each of the various parts being molded by its counterparts, and the whole organism acted upon and acting upon its environment. For example, children with poor psychomotor coordination may have difficulty completing their schoolwork, and consequently become frustrated and suffer a decline in their feelings of self-esteem. The opposite is also possible. Other children who are advanced in psychomotor development may be high achievers in all school skills because of the positive feedback they receive for their psychomotor abilities and their positive feelings of self-esteem. Each developmental component has an interdependent relationship with an individual's other components. As a teacher it is important to respond to the whole, dynamic individual and to allow all persons to interact with their environment in a fashion appropriate for them.

Model of Human Development and Potential

Various models of human development and potential can be proposed using the developmental schemata discussed in this book. Figure 8.1 is one such model. In it the cognitive, affective, and moral developmental sequences of Piaget, Maslow, and Kohlberg are used. These sequences allow human development to be portrayed in three dimensions, as a composite of the three developmental states. It similarly depicts a portion of each person's potential for growth as an interactive phenomenon involving three developmental states. The newborn child may be thought to be in this model at the origin of the three lines, as completely immature cognitively, affectively, and morally. With growing maturity, the child moves further and further from the origin, and closer and closer to the potential.

While cognitive, affective, and moral development are interrelated, their interrelationship does not consist of a one-to-one correspondence. Rather, one developmental sequence may place an upper limit on the others. For example, an individual at Piaget's formal operations stage is not necessarily at Kohlberg's universal-ethical principle stage. However, an individual must possess the cognitive ability to function at the formal operations level in order to achieve Kohlberg's final stages. Likewise, if an individual is functioning at the first or second stage of Kohlberg's hierarchy, this functioning may limit future cognitive development because of the individual's fixed concern about the concrete rewards or punishments to be received. Similar examples may be made using Maslow's hierarchy of needs. In general, while each component of development may place an upper limit upon other developmental components, beneath this limit each component is free to vary.

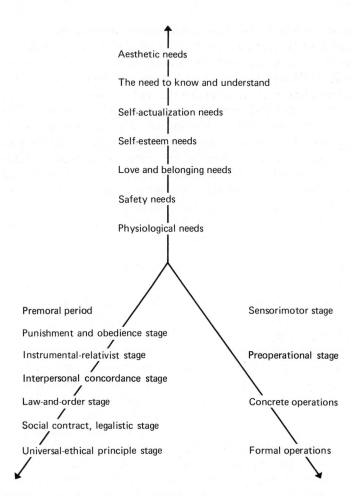

Fig. 8.1   A model of human development and potential.

Individual development cannot be described by just one of the developmental components because of the variability and interaction among components. The model presented in Figure 8.1 was devised to illustrate a more comprehensive view of development. It allows human development to be viewed as a cognitive, affective, and moral process. The similarities and differences among individuals, between individuals and society, and between an individual's present development and future potential for development can all be described in the three-dimensional space of this model. For example, two individuals may both be at the formal operations stage of cognitive development and the law-and-order moral level, but differ in that one is functioning

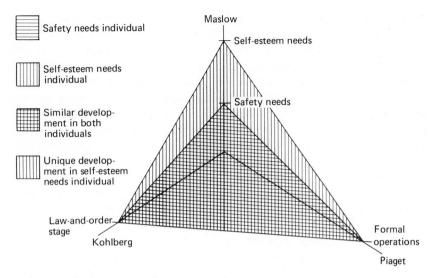

Fig. 8.2 Comparison of the cognitive, affective, and moral development of two individuals.

at a safety needs level, whereas the other is functioning at a self-esteem needs level. The model allows the development of the individuals to be described and compared (See Figure 8.2).

Since the average American adult appears to be at the formal operations cognitive level, the law-and-order moral level, and the love and belonging level of affective needs, a comparison can also be made between the development of an individual and the development of American society through the use of this model. Finally, the model encompasses what is presently known about the cognitive, affective, and moral developmental potential of humans, and thus allows an individual's present developmental state to be compared with future potential development in each of the three dimensions.

Notably, the developmental model just described does not include language development, psychomotor development, or other cognitive and affective developmental sequences contained in this book. The omission of these developmental sequences is not meant to imply that development in these areas is of minor importance. On the contrary, every area of growth in individuals is significant. They were omitted from the model merely to simplify conceptualization of developmental interaction. It is easier to describe, illustrate, and visualize the interdependence of three developmental sequences in three dimensions than n developmental sequences in n dimensions.

The theories of Piaget, Maslow, and Kohlberg were chosen for the model because each describes a different and important aspect of development. Kohlberg's stages may be considered a sequence of moral growth directed toward goodness. This sequence begins with the hedonistic state of premorality and culminates with the transcendent state of moral convictions based on universal rights. Piaget's stages describe growth in cognitive abilities beginning with reflexive actions and concluding with highly abstract reasoning processes. His cognitive-developmental sequence describes growth toward understanding the total environment with which one interacts. Maslow's hierarchy progresses from immediate survival concerns to life-fulfilling concerns. Affective growth can be viewed as developing greater self-understanding and greater satisfaction in life. Together these three theories portray development toward psychological maturity and stability. Combined growth along these dimensions leads to a realistic outlook on life, and a contentment with one's social and personal state.

The origin of the three-dimensional model, relegating the newborn infant to an immature position, may appear negative to many advocates of heredity and/or prenatal development. However, Dewey (1916) clearly articulates that immaturity is not a negative thing because it implies the potential for growth. A newborn infant then characterizes not only the immaturity and dependency with which people enter this world, but also the potential that is inherent within a human being upon first entering life. No one achieves fruition of potential overnight. Rather, the fruition of this potential unfolds as a person passes through life. Similarly, cultures and humankind search and strive for the fruition of the ultimate human potential.

Future Goals for Development

At one time children were thought to be miniature adults, with all adult skills except those limited by their miniature physical size. This belief has faded away, and two developmental schools of thought have emerged. In one school of thought, children are held to have some part of all their potential adult skills. "Any subject can be taught effectively in some intellectually honest form to any child at any stage of development." (Bruner 1966) In the other school of thought, children are held to have particular times in their lives in which skills emerge, like a caterpillar that becomes a butterfly through the process of metamorphosis. Piaget is a proponent of this school of thought. These two different developmental viewpoints, while opening the horizons of thought to possibilities that were inconceivable in the preformationist period, have also been detrimental to future progress in understanding development. Developmentalists have placed these two theoretical positions in diametrical opposition, each school entrenched behind its own significant research aimed at "proving" its particular viewpoint. The research conducted by advocates from both theoretical schools appears to point toward one overwhelming conclusion. Both theoretical positions are valid in some instances, and each is able to adequately explain certain types of development. The area of human development needs a theory which synthesizes and subsumes the significant research from both schools of developmental thought. Einstein went beyond the scientific theory of his time and enabled people to understand more about the world in which they live. What the area of human development needs is a developmentalist who will go beyond the theories presently espoused, and enable people to understand more about themselves. Such understanding will enable people to come closer to achieving full potential. They will then be less the victims of circumstances, and more the tailors of their own vestments and architects of their own destinies.

Until the Einstein of human development emerges, there are still many open, and as yet unopened, vistas of research in development to be explored. Not many in-depth longitudinal studies of the various types of development have been conducted. Nomothetic research of the normative type, in which similarities among large groups of individuals are investigated, has not been carried out in a number of areas of development. Likewise, idiographic research of the clinical type, in which differences among a small number of individuals are examined, is also lacking in many developmental areas. The interrelationships between various known developmental conditions such as cognitive styles have not been analyzed. Generally, besides research into possible but completely unexplored areas of development, the present knowledge of human development in all areas is flawed by many gaps. These gaps must be filled to attain a comprehensive understanding of just a portion of the vast realm of human development.

Educators have still another responsibility. All the knowledge that is presently available about development has not been disseminated to teachers, applied in the creation of curricular materials, or incorporated into the instructional methods used in schools. Present knowledge and research in the area of moral development is an example. Besides developmental stages, types of curriculum materials and teaching methods for moral development have been identified, yet most teachers are not acquainted with Kohlberg's theory of moral development, and the curriculum materials already devised are not being used in most schools. Also, the majority of new materials being produced in this area are not developmentally based, and the teaching methods used in most moral development programs are improper and antiquated, if indeed such a program exists in a school at all. The application of present knowledge about development, then, is critical for future growth toward the human potential.

Thus far in this section of this chapter, future goals for development have been considered with reference to what is already known about development. The discovery of hitherto unknown human abilities and potentials is also a likely possibility. Research presently being conducted in the area of biofeedback is one such possibility in the near future. It appears that individuals who are able to monitor their internal muscular reactions can attain some type of mental control over them. Blood pressure, body temperature, and the secretion of gastric fluid have been successfully regulated by research subjects using monitoring devices. Another possibility is that we humans may have more than five senses, some senses which we have not yet learned to utilize. When one thinks of the amazing advances the human race has made in the last few centuries in all areas of knowledge, the possible developmental discoveries still to be made may be tremendous. Some that may occur are probably beyond our present wildest imaginings.

Previous generations have witnessed great tehnological breakthroughs in the areas of communication, transportation, and automation. In the twentieth century, the car, the airplane, television, and the computer were devised. We have learned to apply our knowledge of our physical environment toward bettering our state in the world. Perhaps it will be in this generation that our knowledge about ourselves will be applied toward bettering the state of people everywhere.

CONCLUSION

Human potential can be approached from many different directions. This chapter has presented three approaches. The first was a model of our present state in reference to our initial state at birth and the known potential of human life. This model may be applied to evaluating the growth of one individual or to comparing the growth of different individuals. It is an approach to our developmental potential which takes into consideration all known types of development and their interactions. The second approach to human potential was from an educational perspective. Individually Guided Education was discussed as a method of aiding students to grow toward their potential. Application of developmental principles is necessary for the human race to reach its potential. The third approach considered development in reference to what is presently unknown or unapplied. This approach to human potential was chosen because it emphasizes what is yet unknown about development. While human potential as presently conceptualized may be within our grasp, it appears that much of the ultimate human potential has still to be discovered.

SUGGESTED READINGS FOR CHAPTER 8

Klausmeier, H. J., J. T. Jeter, M. R. Quilling, and D. A. Frayer 1973. *Individually guided motivation.* Madison, Wisc.: Wisconsin Research and Development Center for Cognitive Learning.

Student motivation can clearly set the road for successful cognitive development. Thus, this report briefly describes the advantages of the four motivational-instructional procedures which have been shown to lead to higher student motivation and educational achievements. The child's cognitive development can be heightened by the procedure of the IGM program including focusing attention on desired objectives, providing observable models, educational goals, feedback, and reinforcement of desired behaviors.

Leonard, G. B. 1968. *Education and ecstasy.* New York: Dell.

Leonard offers to the reader what he considers to be insight into the drawbacks and pitfalls besetting students in contemporary educational settings. He contrasts the misdirected and negative outcomes of contemporary educational practices with what he believes to be more positive and desirable outcomes for students which can be realized in future schools through implementation of recently developed educational methods and devices.

Skinner, B. F. 1962. *Walden two.* New York: Macmillan.

A fictional story about a different type of utopia is constructed upon principles of operant conditioning. Through the characters in this book, Skinner provides answers to many of the criticisms directed at his theory of humans as both manipulators and those who are manipulated.

REFERENCES

Bruner, J. S. 1966. *Toward a theory of instruction.* Cambridge: Belknap Press of Harvard University Press.

Dewey, J. 1916. *Democracy and education.* New York: Macmillan.

Gibran, K. 1923. *The prophet.* New York: Knopf.

Klausmeier, H. J., J. T. Jeter, M. R. Quilling, and D. A. Frayer 1973. *Individually guided motivation.* Madison, Wisc.: Wisconsin Research and Development Center for Cognitive Learning.

Leonard, G. B. 1968. *Education and ecstasy.* New York: Dell.

Skinner, B. F. 1962. *Walden two.* New York: Macmillan.

Glossary

Accountability A dimension of group focus that refers to the degree to which persons are held responsible for their task performance.

Accountability, educational The idea that teachers and school systems may be held responsible for actual improvement in student achievement and that such improvement is measurable.

Affective outcomes of education Results which involve feelings more than understandings. Likes and dislikes, satisfactions and discontents, ideals and values are some of the affective outcomes that education may develop in the individual.

Aide, clerical A paraprofessional whose duties are mainly secretarial.

Aide, instructional A paraprofessional member of the Instructional & Research Unit who, working under the direct supervision of the teachers, performs various routine duties. These duties, which depend on the experiences and skills of the aide, may include working with children in a one-to-one or small group situation, administering and scoring tests, helping students in the media center or on the playground.

Anecdotal method A technique by means of which behavior and responses are recorded, as they occur.

Assessment Application of a measurement procedure; obtaining data through measurement; does not include a judgment and therefore is non-evaluative measurement. Assessment is also used by some writers as a synonym for either evaluation or measurement.

Basic skills Skills such as those involved in reading, language, and arithmetic. Their development is regarded as essential to the further study of content subjects, and they tend to be emphasized during the elementary school years.

Behavior (1) The action or activities of an individual, that is, anything that an individual does, including overt, physical action, internal physiological and emotional processes, and implicit mental activity; (2) Those activities of an organism that can be observed by another organism or by an experimenter's instruments. Included within behavior are verbal reports made about subjective, conscious experiences.

Center, instructional materials (IMC) (1) An area set up by a school system consisting of at least a library and an audiovisual center which contain a variety of instruction material and equipment: *syn.*, educational materials center; multimedia center; learning resource center. (2) An area set aside within a single school in which the multimedia approach is utilized for individual and group teaching-learning activities.

Center, learning An area in the classroom or some designated area in the school where there is a wide assortment of resources for learning.

Cognitive outcomes of education Results from education in the intellectual domain including factual knowledge, comprehension, and various intellectual skills; not to be confused with an *objective* of education, which is a desired result of education.

Competency, functional Ability to apply to practical situations the essential principles and techniques of a particular subject matter field.

Concepts Abstractions based on the properties or relationships common to a class of objects or ideas. Concepts may be of concrete things, e.g., the term "poodle dog" referring to a given variety of dog, or of abstractions, e.g., equality, justice, number, implying relationships common to many different kinds of objects or ideas.

Criterion A standard or norm established as a basis for making qualitative or quantitative comparison.

Criterion, mastery A standard that explicitly indicates full or complete attainment of an objective or objectives, usually in the cognitive or psychomotor domain; e.g., 90 percent on a 30-item test that measures attainment of three objectives in science; walking a mile in 15 minutes without stopping to rest or running. Mastery criteria are usually set when it is known or presumed that one objective, or set of objectives, must be attained fully before the next one can be undertaken successfully.

Criterion, variable A standard that implies that either (a) not all students must attain the same level of knowledge, skill, or affective outcome, or (b) that a particular lesson or unit contains several objectives, not all of which are to be attained to the same specified level. Variable criteria are generally set in connection with expressive objectives, objectives in the affective domain, and objectives in the psychomotor domain. In general, only a limited number of objectives in the skill subjects are to be attained to mastery by all students at one time during their elementary school years, and even here exceptions are made for exceptional students; e.g., blind, deaf, emotionally disturbed, mentally retarded.

Differentiated staffing   Dividing the roles of school personnel into different professional and paraprofessional subroles according to specific functions and duties to be performed in the school and according to particular talents and strengths evident within the human resources of any given school community.

Evaluation   The science of providing information for decision making; the process of delineating, obtaining, and providing useful information for judging decision alternatives.

Evaluation, formative   Evaluation of a student's learning during an instructional sequence; evaluation of an instructional product such as a textbook or film while it is being developed; evaluation of a process while it is being carried out.

Evaluation, of staff   An estimate of the quality of a person's performance based on one or more criteria such as achievement, adjustment, behavior, and the judgment of school officials, parents, students, and the role incumbent.

Evaluation, of an instructional program of a student   An estimate of the quality of the instructional program arranged for a particular student that uses as the criterion the student's attainment of the stated objective(s) of that program.

Evaluation, of student   A process in which information derived from many sources is used to arrive at a value judgment; includes not only identifying the degree to which a student possesses a trait or to which the student's behavior has been modified but also evaluating the desirability and adequacy of these findings.

Evaluation, summative   Evaluation of a student's learning at the end of an instructional sequence (this would also be considered part of the formative evaluation of an instructional program comprised of more than one sequence); evaluation of an instructional product such as a textbook, film, or total instructional program of a student after it is completed or finished; evaluation of a completed process.

Facilitative environments   The intra- and extraorganizational agencies, groups, and individuals who contribute to installation, refinement, and renewal of innovative educational programs.

Group cohesiveness   A condition of a classroom group in which members of a group function as a unit and are free from dissention, conflicting interests, and disrupting forces. Cohesiveness as a group characteristic can be inferred from the attraction the group holds for the members, including resistance to leaving it; the motivation of members to participate in group activities; and the coordination of the efforts of members.

Individually Guided Education (IGE)   A comprehensive form of schooling that is an alternative to the age-graded, self-contained form of schooling; it is designed to produce higher education achievements and to attain other educational objectives through providing well for differences among students in rate of learning, learning style, and other characteristics.

Individually Guided Motivation (IGM) A program for focusing a school's efforts on motivation in accordance with instructional programming for the individual student; four motivational-instructional procedures are designed to increase children's interest in learning related to any curricular area and also to promote their self-direction.

Individualization *See* instruction, individualized.

Inservice teacher education A school system, or area teacher training plan that may include such activities as workshops and seminars for individuals who are already teaching; it is designed to increase staff competency or to inform them of recent developments.

Instruction and Research (I & R) Unit An element of the multiunit school organization typically consisting of a unit leader, three to five staff teachers, an instructional secretary, a teacher aide, and 100–150 students; the I & R Unit replaces the age-graded, self-contained classroom organization for instruction. The staff of the unit is a hierarchically organized team with clearly defined job descriptions.

Instruction, individualized As commonly used, any type of teaching-learning situation in which consideration is given to planning and arranging instruction for the individual student; more strictly, the kind of teaching-learning situation in which each student receives instruction of a different kind or at a different rate from other students; for example, in guided independent study and in proceeding through a sequence of instruction at the individual's own rate; this is in contrast to instructional programming for the individual student in which children who have similar needs and readiness to attain the same objectives are grouped for instruction.

Instructional Improvement Committee (IIC) The organizational element of the multiunit school organization structure at the school level. It is composed of the principal, the unit leaders, and a parent representative. The IIC carries out many planning and evaluating functions regarding instruction previously performed by the principal or teachers independently.

Instructional program (1) A statement or description of instructional activities over a given period of time designed to enable the students to attain specified instructional objectives; (2) that which is being taught or has been taught by the school or teacher in question and the manner of instruction.

Instructional program for an individual student (1) The teaching-learning activities by which the student attains one or more instructional objectives over a short period of time (students with the same needs and readiness may have the same instructional program in a given curriculum area); (2) the combination of all the student's teaching-learning activities in the various curriculum areas for any given period of time.

Instructional Programming Model (IPM)   A seven-step model for planning, carrying out, and evaluating instructional programs for the individual students of a school building (*see* Program, instructional, for the individual student). The model takes into account these conditions: that some but not all instructional objectives should be attained by all students during the elementary school; that some but not all objectives should be attained by students to a criterion of mastery, and that some, but not most, objectives are attained in a fixed and invariant sequence.

Learning   A relatively permanent change in behavior that occurs as the result of practice. Behavior changes due to maturation or temporary conditions of the organism (e.g., fatigue, the influence of drugs, adaptation) are not included.

Learning, independent   Learning that occurs by an individual without assistance from another person.

Maturation   Growth processes in the individual that result in orderly changes in behavior, whose timing and patterning are relatively independent of exercise or experience though they may require a normal environment.

Measurement   A process of assigning numbers to an object or the members of a set.

Measurement, educational   (1) A term indicating the testing, scaling, and appraisal of aspects of the educational process for which measures are available and of the individuals undergoing the educational process; (2) the end product obtained through applying a measure to any aspect of the educational process or the individuals undergoing it.

Motivation   A general term used to indicate the activation and direction of effort, usually toward a goal.

Multiunit school organization   A three-level instructional organizational pattern consisting of the I & R, an Instructional Improvement Committee within the building, and a Systemwide Program Committee within the school district.

Objective, expressive   An instructional objective stated in terms of the kind and/or number of activities to be engaged in.

Objective, educational   An aim stated for education in general, for a school division, or for a subject in general.

Objective, behavioral   An instructional objective that includes a description of observable or measurable behavior; the behavior may be measurable, not necessarily only overt behavior that is directly observable.

Objective, instructional   A statement describing the desired results that may be expected from the particular unit or sequence of instruction.

Paraprofessional   Any person who works within an I & R Unit who is not being employed as a certificated teacher and is not an intern or student teacher; also, see aide, clerical and aide, instructional.

Preservice teacher education   The program planned and implemented by an institution of higher education which terminates in a degree and teacher certification.

Performance   Overt or readily measured behavior, as distinguished from knowledge or information not translated into action.

Programming, instructional, for the individual student   The process of identifying objectives, planning and carrying out a series of related activities and use of materials (learning experience) by which a student is to attain the objectives to a stated criterion; the amount of time may or may not be specified.

Regional IGE Coordinating Council (RICC)   The intermediate group in a three-level organizational arrangement; the group is composed of representatives of the Systemwide Program Committees of the school districts of the region, a representative of the intermediate agency of the region, a representative of at least one teacher education institution of the region, and a representative of the state education agency.

State IGE Coordinating Council (SICC)   The state group in a three-level organizational arrangement; it is chaired by the chief state school officer or a designee, and composed of at least one state IGE coordinator, other key personnel of the state agency, and representatives of each RICC including a teacher educator, a representative of an intermediate agency, and a representative of a Systemwide Program Committee.

Systemwide Program Committee (SPC)   The element of the multiunit school organization at the school district level; it is chaired by the superintendent of schools or a designee and consists of representative central office consultants, principals, unit leaders, teachers, and community representatives.

Team teaching   A type of instructional organization involving teaching personnel and the students assigned to them in which two or more teachers are given joint responsibility for all or a significant part of the instruction of the same group of students; the team may include paraprofessionals and student teachers; the I & R Unit is a hierarchical team with clearly defined roles for all members, and it has functions in addition to instruction.

Test, achievement   An instrument designed to measure a student's accomplishments or proficiency related to some body of knowledge or skill; often used to measure achievement in arithmetic, chemistry, English, typing, and other subjects of study. Most tests made by teachers for classroom use are achievement tests.

Test, criterion   The instrument used to measure the end result of an instructional sequence or an experimental treatment.

Test, mastery   An instrument not intended to indicate how much a student has achieved relative to other students, but only whether or not the student has achieved enough to satisfy the minimum requirements of the teacher or the examining agency.

Index